The Epistle of Christ

Short Sermons For the Sundays of the Year on
Texts from the Epistles

by Fr. Michael Andrew Chapman
Foreword by Fr. John Hunwicke

AROUCA
·PRESS·

Nihil Obstat:
>Sti. Ludovici, die 5. Julii, 1927,
>Joannes Rothensteiner,
>Censor Librorum

Imprimatur:
>Sti. Ludovici, die 6. Julii, 1927,
>✠ Joannes J. Glennon,
>Archiepiscopus

Originally published in 1927
by B. Herder Book Co.

© 2019 by Arouca Press
ISBN: 978-1-9994729-4-8

Arouca Press
PO Box 55003 Bridgeport PO
Waterloo, ON, Canada
N2J 3G0
Send inquiries to info@aroucapress.com

Cover image: "Apostle Paul Preaching in the Ruins" by Giovanni Paolo Pannini (1744)

Cover design and layout: Michael Hamilton

Table of Contents

Foreword ix
First Sunday in Advent 1
    (Romans 13:11) Brethren, knowing that it is now high time for us to rise from sleep.
Second Sunday in Advent 5
    (Romans 15:5) Now the God of comfort grant you to be of one mind towards another, according to Christ Jesus.
Third Sunday in Advent 8
    (Philippians 4:4) Brethren rejoice in the Lord always; again I say, rejoice.
Fourth Sunday in Advent 11
    (Corinthians 4:1) Let man regard us as the ministers of Christ, and the dispensers of the mysteries of God.
Sunday After Christmas 14
    (Galatians 4:4 and part of 5) But when the fullness of the time was come, God sent His Son, made of a woman, made under the law: that He might redeem them who were under the law.
The First Sunday in January 18
    (Acts 4:12) For there is no other Name under heaven given to men, whereby we must be saved.
The Second Sunday in January 21
    (Colossians 3:14) But above all things have charity, which is the bond of perfection.
Second Sunday After Epiphany 25
    (Romans 12:10) Loving one another with the charity of brotherhood, in honor preferring one another.

Third Sunday After Epiphany 28
   (Romans 12: 21) Be not overcome by evil, but overcome evil by good.
Fourth Sunday After Epiphany 31
   (Romans 13:10) Love therefore is the fulfilling of the law.
Fifth Sunday After Epiphany 34
   (Colossians 3:17) All whatsoever you do in word or in work, all things do ye in the name of the Lord Jesus Christ.
Sixth Sunday After Epiphany 37
   (1 Thessalonians 1:2) We give thanks to God for you all, making a remembrance of you in our prayers without ceasing.
Septuagesima 41
   (1 Corinthians 9:24) Brethren, know you not that they that run in a race, all run indeed, but one receiveth the prize?
Sexagesima 44
   (2 Corinthians 12:9) My grace is sufficient for thee: for power is made perfect in infirmity.
Quinquagesima 47
   (Corinthians 13:13) But the greatest of these is charity.
First Sunday in Lent 50
   (2 Corinthians 6:1) Brethren, we exhort you that you receive not the grace of God in vain.
Second Sunday in Lent 53
   (1 Thessalonians 4:3) For this is the will of God, your sanctification.
Third Sunday in Lent 56
   (Ephesians 5:3 and 4) But ... all uncleanness let it not so much as be named among you, ... nor obscenity, nor foolish talking, nor scurrility which is to no purpose.
Fourth Sunday in Lent 59
   (Galatians 4:31) By the freedom wherewith Christ hath made us free.

Passion Sunday..62
    (Hebrews 9:11) Christ being come, a high priest.
Palm Sunday 65
    (A short "Fervorino," which may be added to the announcements or at the end of the reading of the Passion in the Vernacular.)
Easter 66
    (1 Corinthians 5:7) Christ our Pasch is sacrificed, therefore let us feast.
Low Sunday 69
    (1 St. John 5:5) This is the victory that overcometh the world, our faith.
Second Sunday After Easter................................72
    (1 St. Peter 2:25) For you were as sheep going astray: but you are now converted to the Shepherd and Bishop of your souls.
Third Sunday After Easter..................................75
    (St. James 1:21) For so is the will of God, that by well-doing you may put to silence the ignorance of foolish men.
Fourth Sunday After Easter 78
    (St. James 1:20) For the anger of man worketh not in the justice of God.
Fifth Sunday After Easter 81
    (St. James 1:22) Be ye doers of the word, and not hearers only, deceiving your own selves.
Sunday in The Octave of the Ascension.................... 84
    (1 St. Peter 4:10) As every man has received grace, ministering the same one to another: as good stewards of the manifold grace of God.
Pentecost... 87
    (Acts 2:11) We have heard them speak in our own tongues the wonderful works of God.
Feast of the Most Holy Trinity 90
    (Romans 11:36) For of Him, and by Him, and in Him are all things: to Him be glory forever. Amen.

Sunday in The Octave of Corpus Christi 93
> *From the Epistle for the Feast. (1 Corinthians 11:26) For as often as you shall eat this bread, and drink the chalice, you shall show the death of the Lord, until He come.*

Third Sunday After Pentecost 96
> *(1 St. Peter 5:8) Be sober and watch; because your adversary the devil, as a roaring lion, goeth about seeking whom he may devour.*

Fourth Sunday After Pentecost 99
> *(Romans 8:18) Brethren, the sufferings of this time are not worthy to be compared to the glory to come, that shall be revealed in us.*

Fifth Sunday After Pentecost 102
> *(1 St. Peter 3:10) For he that will love life, and see good days, let him refrain his tongue from evil, and lips that they speak no guile (Ps. 33:13 quoted).*

Sixth Sunday After Pentecost..................................... 105
> *(Romans 6:11) So do you also reckon that you are dead indeed to sin, but alive unto God, in Christ Jesus our Lord.*

Seventh Sunday After Pentecost 108
> *(Romans 6:23) For the wages of sin is death. But the grace of God, life everlasting.*

Eighth Sunday After Pentecost 111
> *(Romans 8:12) Brethren, we are debtors, not to the flesh, to live according to the flesh.*

Ninth Sunday After Pentecost 114
> *(1 Corinthians 10:12) Wherefore he that thinketh himself to stand, let him take heed lest he fall.*

Tenth Sunday After Pentecost................................... 118
> *(1 Corinthians 12:11) But all these things one and the same Spirit worketh, dividing to every one according to His will.*

Eleventh Sunday After Pentecost 121
> *(1 Corinthians 15:10) But by the grace of God I am who I am, and His grace in me hath not been void.*

Twelfth Sunday After Pentecost 124
(2 Corinthians 3:5) Not that we are sufficient to think anything of ourselves, as of ourselves: but our sufficiency is of God.

Thirteenth Sunday After Pentecost 127
(Galatians 3:22) But the scripture hath concluded all under sin, that the promise by the faith of Jesus Christ might be given to them that believe.

Fourteenth Sunday After Pentecost 130
(Galatians 5:24) They that are Christ's have crucified their flesh with the vices and concupiscences.

Fifteenth Sunday After Pentecost 133
(Galatians 6:10) Whilst we have time, let us work good to all men, but specially to those who are of the household of the faith.

Sixteenth Sunday After Pentecost 136
(Ephesians 3:19) To know also the charity of Christ, which surpasseth all knowledge…

Seventeenth Sunday After Pentecost 139
(Ephesians 4:5) One Lord, one faith, one baptism.

Eighteenth Sunday After Pentecost 143
(1 Corinthians 1:4) Brethren, I give thanks to my God for you, for the grace of God is given you in Christ Jesus….

Nineteenth Sunday After Pentecost 146
(Ephesians 4:25) Wherefore putting away lying, speak ye the truth every man to his neighbor: for we are members one of another.

Twentieth Sunday After Pentecost 149
(Ephesians 5:15 and 16) See how you walk circumspectly, not as unwise, but as wise; redeeming the time, because the days are evil.

Twenty-First Sunday After Pentecost 152
(Ephesians 6:11) Put you on the armor of God, that you may be able to stand against the deceits of the devil.

Twenty-Second Sunday After Pentecost.................. 155
> *(Philippians 1:6) Brethren, we are confident in the Lord Jesus, that he who hath begun a good work in you will perfect it unto the day of the Lord Jesus.*

Twenty-Third Sunday After Pentecost 158
> *(Philippians 3:20) But our conversation is in heaven ...*

Twenty-Fourth And Last Sunday After Pentecost 162
> *(Colossians 1:14) In whom we have redemption through His blood, the remission of sins.*

Foreword

Evelyn Waugh, in his biography of Mgr Ronald ("Ronnie") Knox, records an anecdote "of doubtful authenticity" about one of the first occasions when that distinguished convert preached as a Catholic priest in the presence of a bishop. The prelate, according to this story, commented afterwards: "An interesting sermon, Father, it was a pity you had to read it". At that time, Anglican clergy commonly wrote their sermons out, while Catholic clergy allowed the Spirit, er, to move them. (Personally, I find that preaching an unscripted homily generally means that I take three times as long to say half as much, and say it very much less well.)

Like the brilliant and witty Knox, Fr Michael Andrew Chapman (1884-1960, priest of the Archdiocese of Indianapolis) was a convert from the Anglican priesthood. His life spanned very nearly the same period as that of Knox; like Knox, he must have honed his ministerial skills in the Anglican Ministry, in which he had spent ten years (1908-1918). That is, Sunday by Sunday he preached, very probably on the Epistle or Gospel of the Sunday. And he wrote his sermons out! So, when such a man made the transit from the Anglican to the Catholic Ministry, he had already preached year by year on the Readings of the old 'Tridentine' Rite. This is because the Epistles and Gospels of the Anglican liturgy were the same readings as those in the Missal of St Pius V, with only a few minor diffeences. They were taken from the Sarum Rite, the medieval English version of the old Roman Liturgy.

And that series of readings, evidenced in the Comes of Würzburg and the Comes of Murbach, probably takes us back to the lectionary system in use at Rome as early as the fifth century. In other words, until the Second Vatican Council, they were the selection of readings which nurtured the piety of clergy and people for a millennium and a half.

The list of books which the Church regards as authentic Scripture, contained in a decree of the Council of Trent, is called "the Canon". Sometimes we hear a phrase "the Canon within the Canon". In other words, the reference is to portions of Scripture deemed to be those most central to the Divine Message of the entire Bible. The phrase is used particularly in Protestant circles of a small group of texts in which the Protestant tradition has considered itself to find its central doctrine of "Justificatio " as that was (mistakenly) understood by the sixteenth century 'Reformers'. This means, of course, that the selection of books regarded as belonging to this Protestant "Canon within the Canon" is purely subjective and idiosyncratic. But I would like to suggest that, for Catholics, there is a Canon within the Canon: and that it consists of those portions of Holy Scripture which by very ancient custom have been publicly read, century by century, year after year, within the Church's Worship.

Because the Bible is the Church's book. The literature within it was written within the Church and for the Church. The Bible was not composed so that individual Christians might read it privately for their personal enlightenment. A great deal of study has been done in academic circles during the last few decades on the relationship between 'Orality' and 'Literacy' in the ancient world. The tendency has been to see the written word as backup for the spoken word in a basically 'oral' culture. (A loose modern parallel might be the cookery book you keep in your kitchen: it is backup for your culinary triumphs.) So the Holy Bible did not drift down word-perfect from the skies;

it emerged from the lived reality of Church life in which it supplied needs and preserved orthodoxy and built up the People of God.

Catholics are often exhorted (I have done it myself) to read the Bible more. They naturally wonder how to go about it. Does one purchase a Bible and then get to work on the first verse of the first chapter of the Book of Genesis ... and then just carry on? I suggest that a better method is to study the passages of Scripture appointed for next Sunday.

We clergy are sometimes tempted to preach mainly upon the Gospel. This is natural: here are the words of Christ Himself, the Incarnate Word; and perhaps the Gospel narratives are a little more vivid than the Epistle readings. So I much welcome this little book as a godsend both to laity and clergy. There is immense wealth in the readings of the Epistles, most of them by that towering intellect St Paul. Perhaps clergy will make its texts the basis of their own homilies, or perhaps they will simply adopt its methods and thereby preach more effectively from the New Testament Epistles.

And I commend it to the laity as a valuable prop in their own study of next Sunday's Epistle!

> John Hunwicke
> *Priest of the Ordinariate of our Lady of Walsingham, sometime Head of Theology at Lancing College and Senior Research Fellow at Pusey House, Oxford.*

First Sunday in Advent

(Romans 13:11) Brethren, knowing that it is now high time for us to rise from sleep.

At the beginning of the new Ecclesiastical Year these words of the Apostle, St. Paul, ring like a trumpet blast in our ears, arousing us to renewed effo ts on behalf of the salvation of our immortal souls. We so easily become careless, the round of routine duties dulls our enthusiasm for religion, we come to take so much as a matter of course that we need, from time to time, some special spur to devotion to quicken our zeal. That is exactly the purpose of such a season as Advent, placing before our minds as it does the eternal truths of our immortal destiny, forcing upon our attention the Four Last Things, Death, Judgment, Hell, and Heaven; calling us to repentance, bidding us prepare for the coming of our King, who is also both our Saviour and our Judge.

(1) A glance at the history of the times just before the birth of our Lord shows us that the world had lapsed into a sad state indeed. It was the time of the greatest splendor of a heathendom, not godless, but having too many gods, and so grown careless even of the great pagan virtues. God's Chosen People had fallen upon evil days, their empire swept from them, their religion (the only true religion in the world) degenerated into a dull formalism, their national spirit all but dead under the heel of the oppressor. To them came St. John the Baptist, the Voice crying in the wilderness, to prepare the way of the Lord, to rekindle the dying hope of a Messias who should deliver

His people from bondage. But so worldly had the Jews become that his message meant to them but the possibility of a return of their temporal greatness, an overthrow of their tyrants, the setting up again of their kingdom on earth. It did not dawn on them that they were in a heavier bondage than that of Caesar, and had need of a Saviour not from their political debasement, but from the infinitely more dreadful slavery of sin. In their selfish pride they felt no need of such a Messias, and so they rejected Him when He came.

(2) The early history of the Catholic Church is the story of the great awakening of the ancient world to a new and better life,—a life founded on teachings and ideals the like of which had never been proclaimed in this world before; a life, moreover, which ran clean contrary to the spirit of the world, against which unceasing battle must be waged, to which no quarter could be given ever. Catholics, to be sure, must live in the world, but they are warned not to be of it. In place of pride, humility was to be cultivated; for the unbridled lust of the flesh crucifixion was decreed, and a standard of purity set up which could only be attained by aid of the supernatural grace of God; for avaricious selfishness, the gentle generosity of charity should transform the world; where the old cruelties of paganism had gone all unthinking of human misery, a multitude of homes and hospitals should minister to the weak and friendless; slavery was to give place to glorious liberty; instead of crass and debasing ignorance, the light of knowledge should be diffused in ever-increasing measure by the institutions of learning which the Faith alone could produce. No persecution could overthrow so vital a force, and almost before the world could recover from its shock of surprise, it was transformed, remade, changed so thoroughly that it was all but impossible to realise what it had been like before.

(3) Yet, in spite of all this supernatural energy, fl wing upon the world from the seven-fold fountains of the Sacra-

ments, human nature, in the mass and in the individual, was slow to shake off its age-long lethargy. The human element in the Church has ever been a drag on the progress of religion, and from time to time special effo ts were necessary to bring home the eternal truths of the Faith to the dull hearts of men. Hardly had the age of persecutions passed, when the giant heresies well nigh disrupted the Church from within. But always in the crisis there was found a clear and powerful voice bidding men shake off the dreamlike trance. Did pride of intellect capture certain leaders, an Athanasius or an Augustine was always ready to step forth and summon men back to the undying Truth. Did too much wealth or power threaten the spirituality of the times, a Francis or an Ignatius would appear with a challenge to simplicity and piety. Did the State, always the embodiment of the arrogance of this world, encroach too closely upon the prerogatives of the Kingdom of Christ, a Hildebrand or a Becket would withstand the assault. So the Church went on, vigorous, alert, ever watchful against anything and everything that might ensnare the souls of men and so rob her of the holy harvest she was sent into this world to reap for God and for Heaven.

Peroration: The story of the individual soul is not so far different from the history of nations. We are all of us far too ready to lapse into a dull formalism, or an even duller worldliness; all too apt to lower the standard of justice and piety; all too prone to slumber and sleep in the soft bed of sin, to put off repentance, to turn our unwary feet into the facile descent that leads to Hell. So to the soul comes, ever and again, one who cries: "Rise thou that sleepest, and arise from the dead, and Christ shall enlighten thee" (Ephesians 5:14). Such a voice comes to each one of us now, at the beginning of Advent, bidding us have done with spiritual sloth and indiffe ence, above all with sin. The practice of the Catholic Religion is not an easy thing; it is hard work for strong men—a man's sized job —requiring great exertion on our part, great alertness against snares, keen conflict against the forces of evil. To this the voice of the Church summons us. God grant that we may heed that voice, and go forth bravely to the task that is ours.

Second Sunday in Advent

(Romans 15:5) Now the God of comfort grant you to be of one mind towards another, according to Christ Jesus.

Unanimity, so much desired by families, societies, nations, can only be had under certain conditions, and at a certain cost, which human nature is not always willing to pay. All men desire peace—they may want it so much that they are willing to fight for it—they may never attain it, but it is always the ideal towards which they struggle; and it can only rule when men are of one heart and mind, one with another, and each one with himself. The ills of the world can, all of them, be traced to sin, which in the last analysis is selfishness. The e can be no unanimity where self is the idol, saved the depraved solidarity of vice which can never satisfy, and certainly never brings peace. One of the great purposes of the coming of Christ was to make all men one in Him. On the eve of His death He prayed that his followers all might be one (St. John 17:11 and 17:21, 22). St. Paul stresses this ideal of unity again and again (cf. Ephesians 2:14, 1 Corinthians 3:4, Philippians 1:26, etc.). Indeed Unity is one of the Marks of the Church, failing which we may be sure that any claim, on the part of any religious body, is false and unsupported.

(1) "Shall two walk together except they be agreed?" asks the Prophet (Amos 3:3). The very first requisite for friendship (whether between individuals or nations) is that they shall think alike on certain important principles. Diffe ences of opinion, of conviction, are fatal; one must agree, ultimately,

with the other, else their ways will inevitably part. It is possible to overlook minor discrepancies in detail, manners, customs, non-essential feelings and desires. But when it comes to principle, the apprehension of Truth, unanimity is essential, failure to arrive at it means rupture, war, unhappiness. In no department of life is this more true than as regards Religion, "One Lord, one faith" declares the Apostle (Ephesians 4:5). Of the first Christians it is recorded that they had but one heart and one soul (Acts 4:32), so close was the unanimity that prevailed among them.

(2) But discord came, with pride and self-working. Heresies crept in, seeking to wreck the Church, which had withstood all possible pressure of persecution from without. Reading history, it may seem to some that the Church was harsh with those who ventured to disagree with her. But it must always be remembered that the Catholic Church is the divinely appointed guardian of Truth; that for all her love and greatness, she must ever face unbelief and sin with uncompromising hostility. Those who will not walk with her, she must, after gentle admonition, sternly reject. After all, it is they, not she, who have broken the bond of peace. The mark of Unity is inherent in her, a part of her nature, an essential of her constitution. She must preserve it, for the sake of the salvation of souls, even at the risk of alienating those who prefer their own headstrong, proud way to her reasonable and peaceful rule.

(3) The spectacle of the disruption and discord of the non-Catholic denominations is the very opposite of the vision of the One Church, forever united and one with itself, upon the impregnable rock of unchanging Truth. If the Religion of Jesus Christ were represented in this world only by the hundreds of warring sects of Protestantism, well might men say it has failed and must soon perish. Christ Himself made the Mark of Unity the proof to the world of His heavenly mission: "that they may be one—and the world may believe that Thou hast seen Me"

(St. John 17:22-23). But it is impossible for an intelligent man, reading the New Testament and history, conversant with the religious life of his own time, to regard the Catholic Church as a mere sect, one of many "divisions of Christendom," itself divided into "branches" which refuse to recognize each other. If you are to have Unity at all, you must have a Center for it; if you admit the principle of One True Church, as taught alike by Bible and History and, indeed, by the very necessities of the case, you cannot justly be accused of either inconsistency or lack of charity if, in recognizing that One True Church, you must adjudge all others false.

Peroration: This spiritual and doctrinal unanimity has ever been the sole possession of the Catholic Church, and alone in the world today she continues to exemplify it. Whatever solidarity of error the various sects had in their beginnings, they have long since lost. Division has given place to subdivision; even in the same sects doctrines and practices, so diverse as to be mutually exclusive, wage bitter warfare; confusion, not peace, is the inevitable and fatal result. "Many men, many minds." No other force than that of truth can unite them. And, as a matter of fact, no other unitive force has ever prevailed over the multitudinous diffe ences of mankind, racial, national, social, temperamental, except the Catholic Religion. It is only in "the household of Faith" that men can be of one mind towards another. It is only in the Unity of the faith that the world or individual can find peace

Third Sunday in Advent

(Philippians 4:4) Brethren rejoice in the Lord always; again I say, rejoice.

No one, surely, should be as happy as the devout Catholic. For the Christian Religion (and when we use that term we mean nothing else than the Catholic Religion) is not a religion of sadness, of grim austerity, of stern repression, but the joy of which our Blessed Lord Himself said, "no man taketh it from you" (St. John 16:22). Even in the midst of her great penitential seasons of Advent and Lent, the Church sounds this note of joy, to remind us that though we rightly sorrow for our sins, yet by God's mercy we are forgiven, and happiness is restored to our hearts. The somber Puritanism which still characterizes so much of non-Catholic Christianity, has no place in Catholic life. The ages of faith were certainly not dark and gloomy, for we know that they were the centuries in which the folk dance and the troubadour flourished, when one of the greatest saints that they produced could call himself "Christ's jongleur," when even the stones of the majestic Gothic cathedrals were upraised with songs of happiness which seemed to crystallize into the gladsome grimace of the gargoyle and the sober, but none the less real, smile of the sculptured saints.

(1) And why should we not be happy? We are Catholics, and therefore need have, and do have, no harassing questions concerning our Faith. Ours is not that sad quest, from one uncertain teacher to another, "searching for truth" (as the saying is) and never knowing surely whether we have found it or not.

Is there not cause for joy in the certitude of Faith, in knowing that the One True Church embraces us in her loving arms, nourishes us with Sacraments, assures us that, if only we do our part, we need never fear for our eternal salvation. True, that salvation must be worked out in fear and trembling lest a man-made foundation and should crumble beneath us, but rather that godly fear lest we might fail, never anxiety for a possible debacle of our religion.

(2) We have Christ for our Saviour and our Friend. In the Most Blessed Sacrament we come, day by day, so close to Him that only one word can describe that intimacy, communion. "Thou shalt fill me with the joy of Thy countenance" (Psalm 15:11); the fullness of joy and happiness is there, more than we can bear in this life. Is any day of our life so filled with joy as our First Communion Day? Surely, as Fr. Faber said, Heaven must be like that, only that Heaven will last always. The e is only one thing that can rob us of that joy, and that is sin, our own or others'. But what shall be said of the happiness of those who have found the way out of the sadness of sin, and by the loving mercy of our Redeemer, been restored to the state of Sanctifying Grace in the Sacrament of Penance? To know that our sins are forgiven, is not that a joy the world can never give? Who is happier than the man who has made a good confession, freed his soul and his heart from the guilt of transgression, stilled the gnawing voice of conscience, made his peace with God?

(3) But you will tell me that, in spite of all this, the world is full of sorrow and suffering, and Catholics certainly have their share of it. What of poverty, what of disappointment, what of disease and death? Of course, we know that these evils are all the results of sin, our own or others'. Absolution does not do away with them, they are an unavoidable part of the temporal punishment that God must lay upon us in this world in order to spare in the next. But even in them there is, for the devout

Catholic, a certain quiet joy, deep down in the heart, for he knows that the patient bearing of them will not fail to bring its reward, and that when sorrow and suffering are our lot, they but draw us nearer to the Sacred Heart, to whom we offer them up. It is this hidden joy which is the secret of the saints, the secret, too, of countless simple souls who have learned to glory in the Cross and to count it joy even when they encounter trials and temptations, knowing that by them their Faith will be perfected (St. James 1:2).

Peroration: In every Mass the priest bids the people "Lift up your hearts,": "Let us give thanks unto the Lord God." These words are said, before the Sanctus, even in Requiem Masses, as if to teach us that the sting of death has been conquered by our Lord, who having joy set before Him, endured the Cross (Hebrews 12:2), that He might fill us with spiritual joy even in our greatest earthly sorrows. They do the Catholic Church no service who set about their religious duties with long faces and make a hardship of the gentle and easy yoke of Christ. If we lived as we ought, frequenting the Sacraments, avoiding sin and its occasions, cultivating the better side of our nature, we would have small room for sadness. Most of the gloom in our lives we make for ourselves, and sometimes for others as well. Should we not rather spread happiness, since God has been so good to us?

We are looking forward to the joy of Christmas, not only the great and solemn religious joy of the commemoration of the Birth of Him who came to banish sadness, but the kindly domestic joy of the season of festivity. We should keep that spirit with us all the year through; we should drink so deep of it that its strength might carry us through difficultie and anxieties with smiling faces. God give us grace so to do!

Fourth Sunday in Advent

(Corinthians 4:1) Let man regard us as the ministers of Christ, and the dispensers of the mysteries of God.

In these words St. Paul sums up the teaching of the Catholic Church regarding the sacred Priesthood. Being a Bishop himself, he knew what the Church held regarding the Sacrament of Holy Orders; being one of the divinely inspired writers of the New Testament, he set forth nothing less than the Truth regarding Priesthood. One might quote passage after passage from his writings to show that the primitive and Catholic conception of the Christian Ministry, the Sacred Priesthood, was the same in Apostolic times as it is today. Yet large numbers of good people, who profess and call themselves Christians, have repudiated this teaching, and in abandoning the Catholic Church, have cast away also every priestly function, and set up a ministry of preaching and social service in its stead. It is well, then, to set forth the principal points of the Catholic conception of the Priesthood, both to refresh our own memories and stir up our own devotion, and also to supply ourselves with such information regarding one of our chief diffeences from non-Catholics as may enable us to give intelligent answers to the questions they so frequently ask.

(1) The Catholic Priest stands before men as the representative of Jesus Christ, clothed with an authority not his own, endowed with powers and prerogatives of a supernatural order, because he has been admitted by Ordination to a share in the Eternal Priesthood of Christ Himself. This is a claim such as no

other ministry has ever made or can make. To our non-Catholic brethren, the ministry is a more or less representative function, derived from the denomination or congregation, by virtue of which an individual is set apart to lead the devotions of the people and to expound to them the Word of God as he understands it. In the nature of the case he can claim, and does claim, no prerogatives or powers which he does not share with the people by whom and from among whom he is chosen. What little authority he has, is delegated to him by them. Not believing in Sacraments, as supernatural vehicles of Divine Grace, working in their own power, his people do not attribute to him any extraordinary powers in the administration of their rites. His influenc is measured by his personal ability, zeal, success in social organization, persuasiveness in preaching, and the like.

(2) The Catholic Priest, on the other hand, is clothed with a dignity and an authority quite apart from his purely personal attainments. The humblest Priest shares with the most prominent the same mysterious gifts, which he exercises on behalf of the people committed to his care by Holy Church. At the Altar he offers up the Holy Sacrifice of the Mass, the highest and most sacred function of his Priesthood. A priest without a sacrifice is a contradiction in terms, as is an altar without a Sacrificing Priest. As the true Minister of Christ, the Priest brings Jesus to us, in that Most Holy Sacrament, wherein He has promised to abide with us through the ages until the end of the world. The power to consecrate the Body and Blood of Christ, to accomplish the transcendent miracle of Transubstantiation, rests not on the personal qualifications of the Priest, but on the almighty power of God. So with all the other Sacraments, "Mysteries of God," as St. Paul calls them. The Priest is their minister, he "confects" them, but the power to do this is from God, and the Grace conveyed by them is of God.

(3) As Ambassadors for Christ (2 Corinthians 5:20), to whom the Great High Priest has delegated certain of His

own divine powers and prerogatives, the Priests of the Catholic Church exercise the Ministry of Reconciliation (ibid. 19) in the Sacrament of Penance, forgiving the sins of those who repent and confess and promise amendment of life. It is this function of the Priesthood which is, perhaps, most difficul for our separated brethren to understand, yet nothing is more clearly taught in the Bible (see St. John 20:2-23) and for twenty centuries the Church has taught this truth which, for fifteen centuries, no Christian dreamed of doubting. So with the other Sacraments, so with the commission to teach in the name of Christ and with the authority of His Church, so with the power to bless in the Name of the Lord, so with the pastoral offic of ruling the Church of God,—all is derived from the power of Jesus Christ, all is done by His express command and under His express commission.

Peroration: We see, then, that in honoring the Priesthood of the Catholic Church, as we do honor and venerate it, both in principle and in practice, even in the person of its least worthy member, we are really honoring Christ, whose institution it is. Like the people in the Gospel, we glorify God, who hath given such power unto men (St. Matthew 9:8). The holy, self-sacrifi - ing lives of our priests call forth our respect and love, but quite aside from personalities, the Priest is the Priest, the Minister of Christ for us, the dispenser of the Mysteries of God to us. If he is a king and loving father, a friend devoted to our best interests, a leader whom we follow with enthusiasm, a teacher to whom we listen with profit to mind and soul, so much the better. But his real offic is far above and beyond these individual and personal attainments, nothing less than that of the representative of Christ to us, and of us before God.

Sunday After Christmas

(Galatians 4:4 and part of 5) But when the fullness of the time was come, God sent His Son, made of a woman, made under the law: that He might redeem them who were under the law.

"Blessed be Jesus Christ, True God and True Man." How often do we say these words, without realizing their tremendous import as the epitome of the great Dogma of the Incarnation. Stripped of all theology, freed from all sentiment, the great fact which we celebrate at this holy season, is that God became Man; that the Second Person of the Ever-adorable Trinity took upon Himself human nature, and, by a miraculous act of the Holy Ghost, the Lord and Giver of Life, was born, as at this time, for us, from the womb of His Virgin Mother. It is, of course, a great mystery. It is, in this age and generation, a hard saying, but it is nevertheless proclaimed as Truth by the Catholic Church, yes, as the foundation truth of Christianity, without which all the rest would be vain and illusory.

(1) For, if Jesus Christ is not God, He can be no Saviour to us. And that, as countless texts of Holy Scripture show us, is the chief purpose of the coming of the Christ Child into this world of sin—to be our Saviour. "Unto you is born—a Saviour," sang the Angel on Christmas Night, and the echo of that song interpenetrated and suffused all that Christ said and did throughout His earthly life. But if He is no more than a man, however good, however perfect, with whatsoever high ideals, proclaiming the most exalted moral and spiritual teaching ever uttered by human lips, He cannot save us from our

sins, He cannot pay to God the Father any the least ransom in atonement for them. Only God could do that; only God could render to God a perfect sacrifice for sin and so purchase the privilege, the right, to blot sin out in His Own cleansing Blood. If Jesus Christ is not God, we have no Saviour, and we are of all men most miserable, for we are still in our sins, and there is no hope for us in Heaven or earth.

(2) If Jesus Christ is not truly Man, He can be no Saviour to us. The e have been, and still are, those who would have us believe that Christ was a sort of phantom, a dream of God projected upon the mind of the world. Neither His Birth nor His death were real, but only seeming, for He was a purely spiritual manifestation, and His religion must be purely spiritual, without any ministration of the things of sense discounting the errors of our mortality. The Church condemned this false teaching in the earliest ages of her guardianship of Divine Truth, but it crops up now and then in the minds of those who fail to realize the inherent dignity of humanity, who look upon the body as in itself an evil thing, who would, so to speak, spiritualize religion out of all practical usefulness. St. John gives us some of the reasons why God became Man, that we might see Him, know Him as friend, love Him with these human hearts of ours, than which no other organ of affection has been given us by God (1 St. John 1:1). St. Paul further explains the mystery by telling us that, in this matter of Redemption, we must have a High Priest who is one of us, who can have compassion—because He Himself also is compassed with infirmity (Hebrews 5:2).

(3) This Truth of the Mystery of the Incarnation, this union of God with man, which we celebrate with so great joy year by year, is the basis upon which rests the whole Catholic and Christian Faith and practice. Without it the Life of Christ is a meaningless failure, the Resurrection an impossibility, the Church a pious fraud, the Sacraments empty

forms, Heaven a dream which can never be realized. Jesus Christ claimed to be God. If He was not; if He was either self-deluded or consciously deluding His followers, what becomes of that perfect character which even "the good agnostics" admit? If He were not God, how explain the infl ence of His life and teachings through two thousand years of history; the survival of the Church He founded, in spite of dungeon, fi e, and sword; the plainly supernatural power of those Sacraments which He instituted as vehicles of His grace, to bring about moral reformation, the upbuilding of character, the nurture of the soul. The unique and elsewhere unknown nature of Catholic sanctity is, by itself, enough to demonstrate the truth of the Incarnation.

Peroration: No other explanation answers all the questions; no other dogma fulfills the necessary conditions; for ages the Church has proclaimed the "good tidings of great joy," and for ages she will continue to transform human life with the knowledge that God has become Man, that Jesus is God, that so we are saved from our sins.

But it has come to pass in our own time that many who profess and call themselves Christians, who keep the outward forms of faith, who extol the morality which Jesus taught, yet deny His claim to Divinity, reject His Virgin Birth, explain away His miracles, criticize His teaching, refuse His Sacraments, while stressing what they are pleased to call "His spirit" in the amelioration of the social and material evils of the world. That He was true Man, they gladly admit. That He was and is true God, they deny explicitly, or vaguely teach generalities regarding their own divinity which rob Him of His unique prerogatives. For them, this blessed Christmastide is a human festival of good cheer and benevolence, a relic of a bygone time when their forefathers held the Faith in its entirety. But to the good Catholic, Christmas is infinitely more than this; it is the confession of the true Faith that God became Man that He might save us; it is the practice of the living Faith that He is with us now, on our altars, in our hearts, our Saviour Friend, our Lord and our God.

The First Sunday In January
Feast of the Holy Name of Jesus

(Acts 4:12) For there is no other Name under heaven given to men, whereby we must be saved.

When Moses, at the burning bush, asked God, who there revealed Himself in a mystery, what His Name was, he was commanded to tell the Israelites that "I AM" had sent him to deliver them from bondage. The Jews spoke of God as Yahweh. But from sheer awe and reverence, the syllables of the Divine Name of God the Father have perished, and it is literally true that we do not know the Name of God which was revealed to Moses.

When the Angel came to Mary to announce the Incarnation of the Second Person of the Ever-Adorable Trinity, he said: "Thou shalt call His name Jesus." This was to be the human name of God, the title by which He should be called, the Name which is above every name, of which it is said that at its utterance every knee shall bow. Yet it was, perhaps, the most common and ordinary of all the proper names in use among the Jews, being the name as Joshua, and meaning, "He shall save his people." That very fact, that it was so common, showed the perfect Humanity of Him who took it, His humility, His desire to be, as much as possible, one of us, in order that He might, indeed, be our Saviour.

(1) Because it is the Name of God Incarnate, true God and true Man, therefore it is clothed with majesty and honor, and worthy of all reverence. If men tremble and fear before the names of the great ones of the earth, how much more should

they honor this Sacred Name of the God-Man. If the signature of the President, or of some powerful individual, gives weight and force to the document upon which it is endorsed, how much more should this Holy Name, which is signed in the Precious Blood of Christ upon the Book of Life, be respected, honored, and loved. Yet, is there any other name in all the world, which is so often used carelessly, thoughtlessly, even irreverently and blasphemously? Strange that evil men do not swear by the name of George Washington, or any other hero of mankind, but by the Name of their Saviour and their God!

(2) To each of us there is some human name which is very dear and precious. It may be the name of Mother, Wife, Sweetheart, or Friend, living or dead. Against that name we will let no one say so much as one derogatory word. We whisper it with affection, we treasure it in memory, we inscribe it upon a costly monument, we love and revere the very sound of it. Yet for the Name which is above every name, for the Name which spells Salvation, for the Name which is sweeter and more dear than any other, we have, all too often, but little regard. If, indeed, we refrain from actual irreverence in our use of the Holy Name of Jesus, how seldom we speak it at all! Yet it ought to be on our lips frequently, with pious affection, else how can we so accustom ourselves to the right use of it that at the moment of death we shall utter it as our passport to Heaven?

(3) Besides the definitely religious reasons for honoring the Sacred Name of Jesus, and for refraining from a profane and irreverent speaking of it, there is another and cogent reason why we should make every effo t to discourage the misuse of it in others, and to train ourselves against carelessness and blasphemy in our own speech. Nothing so marks a man as an uncouth and ill-mannered boor as the habitual use of profane language. A gentleman, to say nothing of a good Catholic Christian, will not so lower himself as to make use of vulgar and blasphemous talk. It always denotes ignorance and poor

breeding. It is never good manners to swear. But the misuse of the name of Jesus is not only positively sinful, but it certainly is not tolerated among men or women who make any pretense of culture and refinement

Peroration: Would to God that you who hear these words might take them to heart! The e are many reproaches brought against our good Catholic people, by those outside the fold, which are unmerited and false. But it is greatly to be feared that the charge of carelessness in this matter of the Holy Name is but too well deserved. You know what effo ts the Church is making to stamp out this abuse.

The Holy Name pledge should be taken by every man and boy in this parish, and every effo t should be made to keep it. It is very largely a matter of habit, and it is perfectly possible for anyone, with an ounce of self-control, to rid himself of a habit of swearing, of which, if he have any manhood at all, he is heartily ashamed. This great Feast of the Holy Name of Jesus stands now at the opening of the New Year. It is certainly not too late to make a good New Year's resolution about this important matter. Shall we not promise our Divine Lord that, with His help, this New Year shall mark—for each one of us—the end of carelessness and blasphemy in our treatment of His Holy Name. We cannot doubt that if we make the effort He will help us.

The Second Sunday in January
Feast of the Holy Family

(Colossians 3:14) But above all things have charity, which is the bond of perfection.

For an instant, in this beautiful feast of Holy Church, the veil which hides the home life of our Blessed Lord, is taken away, and we are affoded a glimpse of the Holy House of Nazareth, where Jesus, Mary, and Joseph dwelt in perfect love and happiness. What a home, the earthly abode of God, shared by the two greatest Saints that the grace of God has ever produced! What a home-life! Hidden though it was, it is the model for all Christian homes. The e was poverty there, but it was not a hardship, for it was patiently borne. The e was hard work there, but it was not, as to the first family of mankind, exiled from Eden, a curse and a bitterness, for by the Incarnation toil was ennobled and made a means of sanctification. What was the secret of the beautiful calm and happiness of the Holy House of Nazareth; how may we, in our own homes, find something approaching to it?

(1) Of course, the very first thought that comes to us, is the key to the whole matter: Jesus was there, and Jesus is, or ought to be, in every Christian home, its center, its inspiration, its guide, at once the source and the focus of the love and kindliness which animates every member of the family, and makes the house a "home." This is not idle verbiage, sentimental mysticism. The presence of Jesus in the Catholic home is very real, and when it is understood, countless blessings must inevitably

follow. He is there because He is God; He is there because He has promised to be with those who love and serve Him; He is there by virtue of His presence in every soul which receives Him sacramentally, and preserves the indwelling presence by keeping free from mortal sin. It is for us to realize His presence, to remind ourselves frequently of the fact, to keep Jesus before our minds, making use of such means as Catholic customs afford to this end, the crucifix, holy pictures, daily prayers by the family gathered together in common worship.

(2) The Holy House of Nazareth was the abode of the divine and mutual love. How Mary and Joseph must have loved the Holy Child! They knew the great secret of God, and worshipped Jesus. Yet, so perfect was the Sacred Humanity of the God-Man, that it is easy for us to picture, as the great artists of the world have loved to do, the human side of the love which permeated the Holy Family. Because they loved each other, not only with divine charity, but with the most pure and perfect human love that can be imagined, therefore they were content with poverty and toil, mutually forbearing, each seeking to outdo the other in those little acts of kindliness which make home life a joy. Can we imagine any one of the inmates of the Holy House as selfish, domineering, inconsiderate of the others? Can we imagine a "family row" in such a home?

(3) But the most profound secret of the Holy House is revealed to us in the text from the Gospel for this feast-day which is read to us in Holy Mass. *Obedience.* That was the key to the happiness, the contentment, the peace, yes, even of the love, which made the Holy Family the model and exemplar of every Catholic household. Jesus was God; Mary and Joseph were His creatures. He was under no obligation to them, under no law, yet he was "subject to them," and that one fact is all that Holy Scripture reports to us of the years of Christ's youth, from the age of twelve until He began His public ministry at thirty. He was obedient, as a boy, as a youth,—voluntarily, perfectly obe-

dient. Humanly speaking, this alone is sufficien to account for the peaceful happiness of the Holy House of Nazareth, and we know, all too well, that there is nothing that destroys the peace and happiness of our own homes so much as disobedience. Humanly speaking, again, Mary and Joseph gave the Holy Child a perfect example of obedience, for their careful observance of the law, both moral and natural is clearly indicated. Joseph was a just man, i.e., he obeyed the law, Mary's whole life may be epitomized in the words she spoke at the Annunciation: "Behold the Handmaid of the Lord."

Peroration: Given a home, however humble and simple, in which dwells a Catholic family, imbued with truly religious principles, living as in the sight of God, frequenting the Sacraments, curbing their passions, in a word, living good Catholic lives. Add to this the mutual love of the several members of such a family, manifesting itself in daily acts of self-denial, consideration, all the little amenities which fl w from the real devotion of human hearts one for another. Crown this with the truly royal virtue of obedience, the obedience of the parents to the law of God, the obedience of the children to the parents, inculcated and enforced as a religious and civic duty; and you will find there a truly happy home, a home which every member of it loves, a home whose influence will go out for good in the neighborhood, yes, in the nation. Multiply that home by thousands, make it the typical Catholic home, and there is no end to the possibilities called up by such a vista.

Is it a dream, this perfect Catholic home life? The Holy Family is not merely an instance of what home life can be, not only an example of what our homes ought to be; the Holy Family makes such homes possible, actually, practically possible. For Jesus is the Source of Grace, by which this desirable end may be reached. Mary and Joseph are our intercessors, procuring for us the grace we need, and must have, to make this dream come true. All that is needed is our co-operation, a good will on our part, an earnest effo t. Shall we let this feast of the Holy Family pass by without at least making a start towards making our homes better and happier and holier?

Second Sunday After Epiphany

(Romans 12:10) Loving one another with the charity of brotherhood, in honor preferring one another.

"The key of all our difficultie " says a famous writer, "is love." It is the theme of all the spiritual masters of the Catholic Church, from the Apostles to the present day. All Dogmatic Theology is summed up in the words: "God so loved the world," and all Moral Theology may be epitomized in the words of the Beloved Apostle: "Beloved, let us love one another." Catholicism, Christianity, is the religion of love, love of God and love of our fellows. St. Paul elsewhere points out how "love is the fulfilling of the Law," and our Lord Himself summed up all the Commandments in the one New Commandment that He gave to His followers, to love God above all things, and our neighbor as ourself. But this love is no mere sentimentality, no vague mysticism; still less is it akin to the unbridled and selfish passion which so often masquerades under the title "love." It is a law, the fundamental law of all relationships, human and divine, the golden bond which "binds us back" to God, and unites us one with another in that fraternal charity which it is upon the conscience of every one of us to observe under pain of sin.

(1) What, then, does this law of charity require of us, and what does it not impose upon us? For this law is both positive and negative, and by implication demands that we shall do certain things and refrain from doing certain other things, if we would obey it in spirit as well as in letter. Perhaps the most

common sin against charity of which we must most frequently accuse ourselves, is "talking about our neighbor" or "making known the faults of others." Now charity, certainly, does not take away our faculty of judgment nor does it require that we should go through life blindfolded, or trying to believe that everybody about us is perfect, when we know perfectly well that they are no more faultless than we are ourselves. We cannot help forming estimates of the character of others, we see what we see, and know what we know, and we have a perfect right to make proper use of that knowledge. But idle gossip, tale-bearing, captious criticism, are not a proper use, and we would do far better to keep such knowledge to ourselves. No one, in this world, is perfect. But no one is utterly devoid of virtues. How much better, since we must, occasionally, speak of others, to study them for good points, and dwell upon them.

(2) Nothing can be more certain, from Holy Scripture and the constant moral teaching of the Church, than the duty of the Catholic Christian to forgive those who have injured him. Our Divine Lord expressly tells us that our own forgiveness at His hands is directly dependent upon our forgiving those who trespass against us. No one would imagine that permitting hate and the desire for revenge to remain in his heart would be consistent with obedience to the law of charity. Yet, there is certainly the plain duty of prudence to protect oneself from the reputation of an injury. One may forgive, without necessarily resuming the active friendship which has been forfeited by the wrong-doing of another, and one may avoid companionship, withhold intimacy, from the person who has shown himself unworthy of trust, without violation of the law of charity. If "to err is human, to forgive divine," it is impossible, and sometimes unadvisable, to forget. If you abandon the very natural wish for revenge, if you wish no harm to those who have injured you, if you freely and fully forgive them (whether they ask it or not), then your con-

science is clear. You need not fall on their necks and weep when next you meet, in order to maintain the law of charity.

(3) But there is a positive side to the law of charity which is even more important than these negative, but highly practical, aspects which we have just considered. Real love for our neighbor will not content itself with doing no ill to him, it will seek to do good, to be of help, both spiritual and temporal. We will, if true love reigns in our hearts, wish others well, and make our wishes come true so far as we can. Both by prayer and by good example we shall seek the spiritual advantage of those we love in Christian charity. Of course, we shall stand ever ready to render temporal assistance when it is needed; those neighborly acts of kindliness which mean so much and cost so little. If we are bound to refrain from injuring others by our talk, we are equally bound to "say a good word" for them when we honestly can and when opportunity offers. Nor will it be necessary for us to go out of our way to find such opportunities. If we really love our neighbor, chances will come to us, constantly, to be of service to him. If we avail ourselves of these opportunities, from a supernatural motive, we shall see that they lead us to the "spiritual and corporal works of mercy" and thus are for the good of our souls.

Peroration: We have a special duty of charity to those who are, as St. Paul says, "of the household of Faith." But the law of charity extends to all, even those "who persecute and calumniate" us. Hard though it may seem to human nature, God gives each of us the grace to keep this, and all His laws perfectly. And it is in the keeping of God's laws, and especially this greatest of them, that true happiness and peace is to be found here in this world, to say nothing of the world to come.

Third Sunday After Epiphany

(Romans 12: 21) Be not overcome by evil, but overcome evil by good.

The greatest problem in life is how to overcome our evil propensities and live a good life. In the solving of this great problem we are not left to our own devices, to blunder along, trying first one experiment and then another, with no sure light to guide us into the ways of virtue and goodness. God, in His mercy, knowing the weakness of our nature, and the many snares that beset us, teaches us how we may win the victory, and the method is so simple that there is no excuse for any of us if we fail to put it into practice. As St. Paul tells us in our text, it is nothing more nor less than crowding the evil out of our life by crowding in the good.

(1) The enemies of the soul, the world, the flesh, and the devil, are busy with the endeavor to crowd evil into our life. They tempt, allure, cajole with false promises of enjoyment, or happiness, or power, sparing nothing in their lifelong effort to rob our souls from God and drag them down to hell. At the very beginning of life we are handicapped by original sin, for we come into this world tainted by this disability, prone to evil, predisposed to sin. But we are not long left under this initial disadvantage, for Holy Church at once begins her work of displacing evil by good, and the Sacrament of Baptism removes the hereditary taint and floods the soul with supernatural, sanctifying grace. As life goes on and we lose that blessed state of grace again and again, the goodness of God again and again

enables us to be rid of sin, to get back into favor with God, to crowd out the evil by flooding our souls with good

(2) As light chases away darkness, so does the grace of God banish evil from our souls. But the conflict between these two forces, good and evil, is lifelong. Well we know that! A thousand unhappy experiences impress the fact of the persistence of our enemies in their unceasing effo ts to ruin us: even more joyful experiences of God's goodness should convince us that, if we do our part, the outcome of that battle can only be victory for the good. We have the assurance of Holy Scripture that we shall never encounter a temptation which we cannot, by God's grace, overcome. We know that no matter how often or how deeply we may fall, through the weakness of our nature and the strength of our spiritual foes, God will welcome us back, pardon our offen - es, reinstate us in His grace, if only we will make the little effo t, form the little act of will, which is necessary in order that we may do our part in the great work of saving our souls.

(3) God is more anxious to save us than the devil is to mislead us into the loss of our souls. If evil abounds in the world, grace much more abounds. If our passions are strong, the supernatural power which God gives us with which to combat them is stronger. For we have, in the Holy Sacraments, nothing less than the strength of God Himself, yes in the Blessed Sacrament we have God, Jesus Christ, the source of all grace, in the most surpassing miracle of grace. Left to ourselves we could not hope to win the battle, with such enemies against us. But, as St. Paul said, "I can do all things in Him, who strengtheneth me." Our Lord Himself warns us, "Without Me you can do nothing." But we know that "all things are possible with God," and if we make full use of the means of grace which He places at our disposal in His Holy Church, we can win, nay, we cannot lose, in the battle of life, the great warfare of the soul.

Peroration: Why, then, should we be discouraged? True, we have often failed, but we have failed because we have trusted in our own strength, because we have not made full use of the aids which God offers us, because we have not given God a chance to show what He can do for our souls. Do you despair of overcoming some bad habit? Have you done everything in your power, used every help of God and Holy Church, prayer, daily Communion, frequent Confession, special devotions, spiritual direction? Have you, in other words, so filled your life with grace, crowded it with holy things, that there has been no room or place left for the evil you wish to overcome? Only when you have done all that, and failed, do you need to be discouraged. But if you do all that, you will not, cannot fail. Of course it takes time and effo t, and yet is it not worth any price, any effo t, any struggle, to save your soul?

Fourth Sunday After Epiphany

(Romans 13:10) Love therefore is the fulfilling of the law.

Asked to select the "great commandment," our Blessed Lord named Love. Love of God and love of neighbor, on these two commandments dependeth the whole law (St. Matthew 22: 40). It was to St. Paul, in the passage which forms the Epistle for this Sunday, to explain more fully just how the Law of Love should ensure the observance of the Ten Commandments. If I love God, I will observe His Day, honor His Name, worship Him as He wills to be worshipped. If I love a person, with a true and worthy love, I will not rob that person, nor kill him, nor do anything by word or deed to injure him. If, on the other hand, I love only myself, I will seek my pleasure and advantage regardless of the rights of God Himself, and such a course will surely lead me into sin.

(1) The human heart is a very mysterious and complicated thing, and human affections and passions form the groundwork of our whole life. It is a great mistake to suppose that you have two hearts,—one to love God, the other to experience those human attachments which make or mar life. In the nature of things, the love we are commanded to give to God, the love which God elicits from us by every claim of benefit and privilege, differs only in degree, not in kind, from the love we give to creatures. It is a spiritual love, but all true and worthy love is spiritual. It is a love which compasses our whole being, ennobling and sanctifying us, but the same should be said of our human loves, or else they are false and

unworthy. The writings of the Saints are full of expressions of their intense love for God, couched in terms that recall the purely human lover. There are those who take exception to this, but they do not understand either theology or psychology; theology, which shows us that God became man in order that He might present to us a Divine object for the love which He demands, which should yet be within the compass of our human faculties and affections: psychology which shows us that, being human, we can only love as human beings even though the object of that human love is divine.

(2) If love for God is exalted and refined and spiritualized, yet still human love, the love which we are commanded to give to our fellowmen is the same kind. God we must love above all things; it suffices if we love our neighbor as ourself (St. Matthew 22:39). It is not merely a question of emotions, for we cannot be expected to have an exactly similar regard for everybody. But it is a matter of duty toward all, even those who have but little consideration for us. We are admonished to love our enemies (St. Matthew 5:44), but surely God, who knows all hearts, cannot expect us to thrill with affection for those who have injured us. It is, then, a matter of the will, which must regulate conduct even against our human inclinations, rather than of feelings which spontaneously arise under favorable circumstances. As true love forbids me to defraud, debauch, kill my friend, so it commands me to refrain from any and all injury to him who has shown himself to be my enemy. Not only must I regulate my external conduct according to the law of charity, but I must even seek to control my interior feelings, and so "pray for them that persecute and calumniate" me (St. Matthew 5:44).

(3) True and worthy love is the exact opposite of selfish-ness. But there are emotions and passions, often wrongly called "love," that are thoroughly selfish, that seek only gratification of self, often at the expense of others.

St. Paul gives us the test of true love: unselfish, devoted to the interests of others rather than our own, willing and eager to suffer and make sacrifices, seeking always the good of the beloved at whatever cost to self (1 Corinthians 13:1-7). It is true, we are not angels, pure spirits, but inseparably compounded of soul and body. And the body has its pure and blameless part to play in all our love, both for God and for men, But in both it is a subordinate part, that, merely, of expressing the high and holy and spiritual love of the soul. The human and physical element in love is to be controlled by the will, kept within the bounds decreed by law, never permitted to forget its place or to debase the pure and disinterested love of the soul into the inordinate passion of self-seeking. Every breaking of a Commandment is an insult to true love, a setting up of self upon the throne where God, who is Love, should rule supreme.

Peroration: Full well we know how difficult of attainment is such a high ideal. God knows it, too, for He has made us as we are. So He gives us the grace, which alone can make it possible for us to love Him as we ought. Such love is, as St. John tells us, of God (1 St. John 4:7). It is a divine virtue infused in Baptism and only the continued grace of God can preserve it unsullied in our souls. It manifests itself in what we call "a good life," in the keeping of the Commandments, in constant self-sacrifice, in the restraint of base passions, in the temperate use of all things, in the firm setting of the will against all that is evil and contrary to God's will. That divine virtue is ours, by Baptism, by every Sacrament since received; ours to exercise, ours to treasure and conserve, ours to increase daily more and more, to our true happiness here in this world, and our ever-lasting reward in the life to come.

Fifth Sunday After Epiphany

(Colossians 3:17) All whatsoever you do in word or in work, all things do ye in the name of the Lord Jesus Christ.

"All that I am, all that I have, Thou O Lord hast bestowed upon me, therefore I give back all to Thee" Thus St. Ignatius in that wonderful prayer, the "Suscipe," in which he teaches us to offer every thought, word, and action to God, in fulfil ment of the Apostolic precept. As a simple matter of justice we are bound to make this offering of our life to God, for our life belongs to God, since He created us, and we have nothing of our own to render to Him in gratitude for the gift of life. Indeed, it is precisely in order that we may live to God's honor and glory that life is given to us at all. Every other purpose is subservient to this one great end, the glory of God and the salvation of our souls in which, so far as we are concerned, God's glory is best served.

(1) The practical Catholic begins each day of his life by making an offering to God of himself and all that he will do or say or think during that day. In this way he blesses and sanctifies his every moment and by intention dedicates it and places it under the protection of God. All that he then does is, by that intention, supernaturalized and becomes a good work. He may not advert to this fact often during the day, but the more often he does so, renewing his offering, then less likely will he be to permit anything to enter into his day's doings which would be unworthy of the blessing of God. If there arises some crisis, if he is called upon to suffer in mind or body, if trouble or sorrow or sickness comes, these, too, he

will offer up, and thus make them meritorious for the good of his soul. There is nothing too great to offer to God in this simple way, nor is anything too small and trivial to form a part of this constant-ly renewed offering. "Who sweeps a room as in God's sight, makes that and the action fine," says a great poet.

(2) The e is only one thing which cannot be offe ed to God, and that is sin. For sin is the exact opposite of offering to God the whole powers of our bodies and minds; sin is robbing Him of their services which is His due; sin is alienating them from their proper function as ministrants to our salvation, and turning them into instruments of damnation. Sin is disobedience. By sin we break the golden chain that binds us to the feet of God as His humble and loving servants. Nor can we pick and choose as to what we will give to God, surrendering part, withholding part. We cannot dedicate our words to God and give our thoughts to evil; we cannot offer some of our acts to Him and turn over other acts to the enemies of the soul, the world, the flesh, and the devil

(3) Yet is not this what so many people try to do? They would not dream of abandoning God altogether, yet they seem to think that they can take a vacation from serving Him at times, or that they can satisfy their duty by giving Him a half-hearted or partial service. As who should say, I will be a good Catholic from six in the morning until noon, but the less said about what I do from noon till midnight, the better!" Or (that you may see the absurdity of this matter more clearly): "I will keep the first and fifth commandments, but not the second and sixth!" Now is not that practically what some to us seem to be saying instead of making the complete offering of our whole obedience to God?

Peroration: Of course God, who has the right to our entire allegiance, our whole life, our complete obedience, will not be satisfied with any such partial and imperfect service. And we ought not to be satisfied with it either. Where it is a matter of relation of other human beings to us we are not content with any halfway arrangements. What parent is satisfied with half-obedience from his children? What lover is content with the half-hearted affection of the one he loves? What business man will tolerate half-service from his employees? Who of us feels secure in a half-loyalty on the part of his friends? Even in our human sense of justice and the fitness of things we demand "all or nothing." True, there is the old saying that "half a loaf is better than no bread"; but half a loaf is robbery when you are entitled to the whole. And God is entitled to our whole and individual and undivided service. More than this, he demands it, and we shall have to reckon with Him if we refuse to give it. But if, gladly and willingly, we make the surrender of ourselves to Him, he will give us the grace we need in order to make that offering constantly. He will protect His own. And in that voluntary service of God we shall find life happier, more effective, more successful, more livable, than ever it could be while we tear ourselves apart striving to serve two masters.

Sixth Sunday After Epiphany

(1 Thessalonians 1:2) We give thanks to God for you all, making a remembrance of you in our prayers without ceasing.

Among the duties and privileges of Catholic life prayer is at once the most common and the most neglected. We all know that prayer is a duty; we were taught to "say our prayers" at our mother's knee; certain times were set apart for prayer all through our school days; and he would be an ignorant Catholic indeed who did not know that he ought to raise his heart to God in prayer at least every morning and every evening of his life. We are supposed to pray when we attend Holy Mass; we are admonished to pray in any and every crisis of life; when in danger, when tempted, when death threatens. Yet what duty of our holy religion is more frequently neglected? How few of us ever go to confession without having to mention that we have omitted our morning or nights prayers a few times; how often we must admit, with shame, that we have prayed carelessly and with willful distractions.

(1) One reason for this remissness is that we forget that prayer is not only a duty but a privilege. We look upon it as a task, a routine to be gotten through with as quickly as possible. Rather we should consider it, next to the offering of the Holy Sacrifice and the reception of the Sacraments, as the highest act of which our minds and hearts are capable. Think what it means to pray, and to pray well. The little child in Catechism will tell you that praying is talking to God. Talking with God! What a stupendous thought! That I, a creature, may hold converse with

my Creator; that I, a sinner, may yet come into the presence of Him who has redeemed me, and speak to Him as a friend! Were I permitted an audience with the Pope, the Bishop, the President, or some great man, would I not be elated by the anticipation of so great an honor, gratified at the time, and never weary of telling of it afterwards? "When I was in Rome," you would say, with pardonable pride, "I had an audience with the Holy Father, and talked with him for fifteen minutes." But, when I was in church this morning, I had an audience with Jesus Christ, and I looked around, and ruffle the leaves of my prayer book, and twirled my beads, and said not one word to Him, though I was there for half an hour.

(2) Think of the marvelous condescension of God in permitting us to approach Him and speak to Him. The great ones of the earth are very choice as to whom they will admit into the circle of their friendship. The e are people in this very city or town with whom I would like to talk, but they do not know me, as the saying is. Yet God is available to the most humble, nay, to the worst and most needy more accessible than to the rich and powerful. He is never too busy to attend to our little concerns, never too angry to heed our cry for mercy. He even invites our confidences and our petitions; indeed it is His command that we present them, regularly and faithfully, and never doubting but that He will hear us, and grant us our request if they be for the good of our souls. Yet, although we believe all this, we somehow are very slow to put it into practice. Even when we "say our prayers" how seldom we really pray! Rather we repeat certain forms, read a page or two in our prayer book, bless ourselves, and think our duty done. Though we may have formally performed our duty, we have certainly not risen to the great privilege of prayer, and it is small wonder that our devotions are but a task.

(3) Another reason why our prayers are so unsatisfactory, both to God and to ourselves, is that they are, all too often,

selfish. We ask and ask for those things that are requisite and necessary as well as for the body as the soul, for temporal blessings and spiritual favors; but when God has graciously granted our petition, we forget to thank Him. But thanksgiving is an essential part of prayer, without which it is imperfect and but half complete. We have so many reasons to be thankful to God, and, it may be supposed, we really are grateful to Him for what He has done for us. Very well then, tell Him so! What do you think of a friend, for whom you have done some favor, who neglects to thank you for it in a mannerly way? He may not be effusi e, but you at least expect due acknowledgement of your kindness. If he turns away silent, or with a perfunctory and curt "Thanks!" you may say, "Well, it will be a long time before I go out of my way for him again." Not that God is annoyed by our ingratitude, but that we should be ashamed of it.

Peroration: Not only in the text which stands at the beginning of this sermon, but in many others, St. Paul (and other Apostolic writers) link prayer and thanksgiving as complementary parts of one act of worship. Holy Mass itself, the great act of prayer and sacrifice, is called the Holy Eucharist, meaning (from the Greek), thanksgiving. Commentators re-mark that our text is an assurance to the Catholics of Thes-salonica that the Apostle was frequently saying Mass for their intention as well as praying for them personally. It is a signifi-cant fact (to which any priest can bear witness) that, although our people are very careful to have Masses said for their pri-vate intentions when they wish to secure some favor from God, it is comparatively rare for them to ask that a Mass of thanksgiving be said in gratitude for favors received. And how seldom do we spend time in prayers of thanksgiving, even after we have received Holy Communion, for which we may have made a careful preparation! Yet our whole life should be one long song of praise to God for what He has done and is doing for us. How can we thank Him enough? The least we can do is to acknowledge His Beneficence in our prayers, and by securing the offering of the great sacrifice of thanksgiving we may be sure that our gratitude is adequately expressed.

Septuagesima

(1 Corinthians 9:24) Brethren, know you not that they that run in a race, all run indeed, but one receiveth the prize?

The famous athletic contest of the ancient world furnished St. Paul with many illustrations of the Christian life. He likens the Christian, striving against sin, to the wrestler, or boxer, who trains himself by an abstemious regimen to meet his opponent. The Christian course, he tells us, resembles a race but the prize, instead of a withering crown of olive leaves, is the imperishable crown of eternal life. The similitude is not only picturesque, but very practical. Think of the athlete, of our own day or of ancient times, how engrossed he is in the contest before him, what sacrifices he is willing to make in order to take his place in the field, with what interest and zeal he plays his part, and with what satisfaction and happiness he receives the reward of his winning.

(1) When you read in the sporting page of your daily paper, of the success of this or that athlete, victorious over all contestors, winner of a title, maker of a new record for speed, or endurance; when you look at the pictures of splendid manhood or womanhood in the persons of champions in the various sports, do you stop to think of how that man or woman won the coveted place? Months, it may be years, of hard work, grueling training, constant practice that led up to the final success-ful result of the contest. Regular hours, simple meals, constant self-denial,—all that is comprised in the word "training",—were necessary to bring that bodily machinery into condition to take part in the sport. Mere strength alone could not win, but muscles must be trained,

the fine points of the game or match made almost instinctive, constant practice, unremitting toil, hardships patiently borne—for what? To win a title which will be forgotten, a prize which will soon be worthless, a name which men will praise just so long as it is the name of the champion, and forget as soon as the title passes to another.

(2) As a nation, we love sport. The successful boxer or foot-ball star, the winner of a famous race, is temporarily a hero in the eyes of old and young alike. It could hardly be said that our enthusiasm for athletics is based entirely upon a desire to bring up a race of physically perfect men and women. We like to win, and the winner is the favorite, while the loser is always unpopular. Most of us take our athletics from the grandstand, but many a man past his prime, and many a woman who fears for her good looks, is exercising and dieting in the hope of im-proving the condition of the body. As the athlete is willing to endure all sorts of hardships for the sake of winning his game, so are most people willing to spend time and money and effort to attain and keep physical health.

(3) As the soul's health is infinitely more important than that of the body so is the contest of the soul, by which it wins the eternal crown of glory, inestimably more important than any race, or match, or game that draws thousands of spectators to the stadium. And in this spiritual contest there are rules, training, practice, the rush and excitement of the fight, the chance of displaying skill, and, not least, the crown of victory to be gained. The field upon which we engage in the race is the course of life. The saints and angels are the "innumerable cloud of witnesses." Christ Himself stands at the goal to present the crown of fadeless worth and beauty to the victors. But there is this difference, that while in the contests of sport there can only be one winner, in this spiritual contest we can all be winners, by the help of God. The man who loses a game still keeps the physical fitness which his training gave him, the skill which

keeps the physical fitness which his training gave him, the skill which long practice brought to him, the respect which all must feel for what we call "a good loser." But the man who loses in the spiritual contest, loses everything, for it is eternal life that is at stake, salvation which is the goal, the eternal happiness of Heaven that is the prize.

Peroration: The Holy Gospel for this Sunday also has a parable concerning the reward which awaits the faithful servants of God. As is often the case, the lesson of the Epistle and of the Gospel is the same. But only one point is called to your attention in conclusion, the utter and entire disproportion between the effo t and the reward. For the reward is the free gift of God; a life of constant effo t, unremitting self-denial, ceaseless figh - ing against temptation, perpetual penance for sins committed, would be all too cheap a price to pay for Heaven. But just as the daysman in the Gospel pays the last laborer as much as the first, so the prize at the end of the race is far exceeding the due of the runner. It is for us to make the effo t, to run the race with skill and patience, and to trust to God for the reward. So may we, at the close of life, say with St. Paul, "I have finished my course—as to the rest, there is laid up for me a crown of justice."

Sexagesima

(2 Corinthians 12:9) My grace is sufficient for thee: for power is made perfect in infirmity.

"Man's extremity," it has been said, "is God's opportunity." If there is one thing which experience teaches us, it is the infallible truth of Christ's dictum, "Without Me you can do nothing." Yet, such is the pride and perversity of human nature, that it takes a great deal of experience to teach us the lesson of our own weakness and helplessness, the utter impossibility of living a truly good life, overcoming temptation, mastering passion, without the supernatural help from God which we call divine grace. We do not like to be dependent upon anyone, even God. We do not like to admit our weakness, even to ourselves. And so our pride goes before every fall, and it is only when it is too late that we realize our mistake in trusting to the strength of our own character, which proves but a slender protection against the assaults of the enemies of the soul.

(1) We have but to look about us at the world in which we live, to realize how impossible it would be for us to live good lives were it not for help of God. For the world has gone mad, mad with greed, ambition, pride, pleasure. Worse than this, it has forgotten God, or where it does remember, choses to ignore Him. Yet it is in this world that we have to live, in it, but not of it, and our Blessed Lord Himself has warned us that for this very reason the world will hate us, and do all that it can to ensnare us to our ruin (St. John 15:19). We see the wicked successful, the dishonest becoming rich, the libertine admired, the irreligious prosperous and respected; we even see people who have no

religion at all living apparently good lives, while many a saint of God is poor, a failure (as the world counts such things) beset with trials and troubles, afflicted, forsaken. How easy it is to yield to the lure of the world, to trust to the world for the power and success which seem to result from merely following the crowd. Yet a moment's reflection will suffice to dispel this false reasoning, to show us that, unless God help us, we yield to the world at the peril of our eternal salvation.

(2) Who of us does not know the terrible power of temp-tations of the flesh and realize how weak are our efforts to overcome them? The very fact that there is a right and natural and lawful use of bodily pleasure makes it all the more difficult to resist the temptation to make use of it in wrong and unnatural and unlawful ways. Once unbridled, there is nothing harder to subdue than our passions. Nor do all our tempta-tions come from without, for the flesh is an enemy that lurks within the citadel, and it is literally true that a man's worst foe is himself. Since this is true, how foolish to expect to conquer self by self-help alone! We must have help, help from outside, help from one stronger than ourselves. And there is only one power mighty enough to overcome our all but overmastering passions, and that is the grace of God.

(3) One of the cleverest plots of the devil to get men into his clutches is to persuade them to disbelief in his existence! For if there were no devil, why fear him, why fortify oneself against him, why renounce him and all his works? Be warned! The devil is not dead, but still seeks souls to drag them with him into Hell. His is the malice of implacable hate, the skill of an age-long knowledge of man's weakness. As the "father of lies," his policy is to deceive us, and one of his pet deceptions is making us believe that we can, unaided and alone, produce a strong and upright character.

Peroration: With such an array of enemies, we might well cry out with the Apostle: "For these things who is sufficie " (2 Corinthians 2:16)? How can we escape, how can we hope to overcome, how, then, shall we be saved? But it is when, and only when, we realize our need, that we are ready to make full use of the grace which God sends to succor and help us. We know that God sends to each of us enough grace, and of the proper and appropriate kind, to enable us to overcome all temptations, however strong or persistent that may be. When we fail, we fail because we do not use the grace God gives, and we do not use it, because, God help us, we do not feel the need of it. Success, in the spiritual life; victory, in the spiritual conflict, lies in the realization of our own need, and the use of the help which God gives to supply that need. We must not be discouraged at the thought of our own weakness, nor by the power of temptation brought against us. We must not trust in ourselves, but in Christ who strengthens us. With his help we can overcome our enemies, by His grace, used faithfully and fully, we shall be saved.

Quinquagesima

(Corinthians 13:13) But the greatest of these is charity.

Is there a word in all our language so much abused and misused as the word "Love"? St. Paul gives us the true, and inspired, definition of the word in the Epistle for this Sunday,—a touchstone by which we may test our emotions, a criterion by which we may judge ourselves in our relations to others, a standard in comparison with which we may recognize the false from the real, and know whether or not we are keeping the commandment of our Blessed Lord, to love God with all our heart and strength, and our neighbor as ourself. If we take but three aspects, or notes, of this greatest of virtues, for our theme today, it is only because the subject is so rich that some selection must be made or, like some of the saints, our discourse would be forever on Love!

(1) It is evident, from the words of our Lord, from the teaching of the Apostles, from the age-long doctrine of the Catholic Church, that the only sufficien motive for good works is love, love of God, and love of our neighbor. St. Paul, in this Epistle, puts it succinctly when he says that the distribution of a man's entire estate in what we are wont to call "charity" is of no avail if the motive of love is absent. He might do it through human respect, to gain the good opinion of men. He might do it because the sight of want and suffering was distasteful to him. He might do it through fear, or for any number of motives other than love, and it would profit him nothing for his soul's welfare. In doing our good deeds, in giving our mite to the various

charitable objects proposed to us from time to time, we must search and purify our motive if we wish to gain merit by our good deeds.

(2) The list of the qualities or attributes of true love, which St. Paul enumerates, leaves us in no manner of doubt as to the utterly unselfish character which is the ultimate test of sincere charity towards God or towards the neighbor. That little phrase, "seeketh not her own," means more than simple altruism, admirable though that quality may be, Our Lord's admonition to those who give alms is:

"Let not thy left hand know what thy right hand doth" (St. Matthew 6:3), and He tells us that those who claim their recompense for almsgiving in this world need expect no further reward in the next. It is the quiet, unostentatious, anonymous doer-of-good, with the motive of pure unselfish love, whose good deeds will await him, loaded with merits, beyond the gate of death.

(3) The great patience of true love, epitomized by St. Paul in this Epistle, shows us how far short we fall in our practice of this virtue. How we shrink from proving our love for God, by the preserving practice of those things in our Religion which "go against the grain." How easily we are discouraged in our dealings with one another. So ready to take offense, so slow to forgive, so unwilling to make the effo t to understand the point of view of others, to find extenuating excuses for their failure to do what we think they ought to do. How many friendships have been wrecked on the rock of pride, because one would not say: "I'm sorry" or the other would not accept an apology for some little wrong or misunderstanding. That is because we think first of ourselves, and are so impatient of anything that crosses our own will and desire.

Peroration: We shall miss the whole point of St. Paul's discourse on love if we fail to remind ourselves that this "charity" of which he speaks, and which we have been trying today to understand better, is a supernatural gift, a "theological virtue," something beyond the power of human nature to practise without the grace and help of God. But we have, all of us, this gift. It was infused into our souls in Baptism, and so long as we preserve the state of sanctifying grace, it is possible for us to exercise the gift of charity in our relations with God and with our fellowmen. By sin, we lose this gift, to regain it only by penance. What wonder, then, that once sin has entered in to spoil our life, we fail so completely to measure up to the standard of love which can only be realized by the grace and help of God. The only way in which we can assure ourselves of making even a beginning in the practice of this surpassing virtue is by keeping ourselves in the state of grace. This is true of faith, it is true of hope, it is trebly true of love. Therefore it is that Holy Church, in teaching us, on this day, the lesson of love, bids us pray to God to "unloose the bonds of our sins" (Oration for Quinquagesima) that we may so be free to love, truly, supernaturally, unselfishly, patiently, and so gain love's eternal reward and fruition at the last.

First Sunday in Lent

(2 Corinthians 6:1) Brethren, we exhort you that you receive not the grace of God in vain.

It is a terrible thought that man can frustrate the grace of God, block its operations in his soul, make it of no effect When we think of God's mercy and goodness in supplying us with such unbounded streams of grace, pouring out upon us so many favors, giving us such opportunities to fulfill the destiny of our life, (which is, to save our souls)—and then, contrasted to that, our tepidity, our carelessness, our remissness in the use of grace, we may well be alarmed and disquieted. At such a time as this, the beginning of the holy season of Lent, we may well devote a few moments to stirring up within ourselves the proper dispositions for the reception and use of the manifold graces which God bestows upon us at this and all times.

(1) While it is true that the Sacraments bring grace to the soul *ex opere operato*, it is no less true that the effects of that grace are enhanced by worthy reception, and by correspondence with it on the part of the recipient. The dispositions of a person approaching any Sacrament have a great deal to do with the effect, the result, the fruits, of its reception: as, for example, penance, to be effective at all, must be received at least with contrition, and, unworthily received, fails entirely of its purpose, nay more, has an effect which is the direct opposite to the grace of absolution, and so far from freeing the soul from sin, plunges it into even greater guilt. The Blessed Sacrament must be received under certain

conditions. If these are absent, the Communion is what we call "bad," and instead of nurtur-ing the soul and flooding it with grace, makes its condition a thousandfold worse than it was before.

(2) The sacramentals, prayer, and what we might call "the other means of grace," work *ex opere operantis*, and their ef-ficacy is definitely determined by the use the recipient makes of them. In all this the responsibility of those who receive any grace at the hands of God is quite plain. If we accept His favors, we are bound to do so with the proper dispositions, and to make use of them to the very best of our ability. Thank God, unworthy reception of the Sacraments, that is to say, failure to conform with the formal conditions, is very rare. Of course, only the Saints receive them worthily in anything like the strict sense of the word. But certainly we ought not be content with merely fulfilling the required conditions for receiving the Sac-raments. The better preparation we make before going to any Sacrament, the more benefit we shall have from it. The more we treasure and use the grace of the Sacraments received, the more will that grace affect our whole life.

(3) So often we are inclined to keep the bare letter of the law, to receive the Sacraments with a certain formalism which does not, to be sure, render them ineffectual, but which cer-tainly does deprive us of the full measure of benefit which we ought to derive from them. If we place no obstacle in the way of the workings of divine grace, we shall experience its effects, no doubt. But if we prepare ourselves with care for that reception, if, after having received the Sacrament, we spend some time in thanking God for His gift; if we make a conscious effort to use the grace bestowed, adverting to it frequently, stirring up our affections and our will to correspond with the favor God has given, may we not feel sure of a greater blessing than would be ours if we prepared perfunctorily, received with cool-ness or out of routine, and then forgot all about it?

Peroration: But the Sacraments, as we well know, are not the only "means of grace" offe ed us by the mercy of God. In many ways, spiritual opportunity knocks at our door, not once, but often. Such an opportunity is this holy season now beginning, with its extra services, its sermons, to stir to renewed devotion, to more sincere endeavor, to greater holiness of life. While we are not bound by any law of the Church to assist at Holy Mass more frequently during Lent than at any other time, while we are under no strict obligation to hear sermons, or take part in other devotions of the season, while even the rules of fasting are relaxed in many cases, ought we not to regard Lent as a chance, an opportunity, a privilege, a time when we may come closer to God, and let God come closer to us? If God offers us, as He certainly does, special favors during this season, is it not "up to us" to appropriate them, to avail ourselves of His gifts, to spend this Lent, not waste it in vain?

Second Sunday in Lent

(1 Thessalonians 4:3) For this is the will of God, your sanctification.

That is the great universal vocation of all of us,—to save and sanctify our immortal souls. We may be in doubt about other aims and purposes of life, but about this paramount intention of God, which ought to be our first intention as well, there can never be the shadow of a question. A man may not know at once, for example, whether he ought to enter upon this or that business venture. But he always knows that he must not enter upon a career of sin. A child may not know, again, for example, whether he ought to become a priest, or she ought to enter Religion. But even a child knows that God wants him to be good and holy. We are all of us called to be Saints. We know, with the certitude of faith, which is the strongest of all convictions and the clearest of all knowledge, that God wills us to be saved, that God wills us to be holy, that God wills us to avoid sin and its occasions.

(1) Reason alone would tell any thinking man that God, who is all-good, would wish His creatures also to be good. Revelation, supplementing and completing reason, gives us the words of God Himself, "By ye holy, because I the Lord your God am holy" (Leviticus 19:2). Holiness is one of the "notes" or marks by which the true Church may be recog-nized, and the holiness of her members is her chief concern, one might say that, next to the glory of God, it is for the sanc-tification of men that the Church exists. Yes, God has made His will very plain and clear in this matter, and nobody but the most perverted and blind enemy of God would dare to say that He wills otherwise

than that His children should be sanctified and saved.

(2) Sin is deliberate disobedience to the known will of God. In the Catholic Church we are left in no manner of uncertainty as to what God forbids in the moral realm, for His Commandments, and those of His Church, are inculcated from our earliest years. If we go wrong, we cannot honestly plead ignorance. The Commandments are both positive and negative, "thou shalt" and "thou shalt not." But our wills are free, free to obey, free to disobey, else where would be the merit of obedience, or the guilt of refusing to observe what God commands? So long as we submit our wills to the all-holy will of God, we are safe. Nor is this submission unworthy of us, for we are creatures, and, as the poet has said, "our wills are ours, to make them Thine" To conform our human wills to the Divine Will is the highest act of volition of which we are capable.

(3) But, because we are human, because our nature is a fallen nature, because we live in the world, in the midst of temptations, because there are enemies of our souls whose whole effo t is to deflect our wills from the service of God, therefore obedience becomes our most difficul task, a task which, indeed, would be impossible were it not for the help which God gives us to enable us to be holy. This help of God comes to us in many ways, in the holy Sacraments, in answer to prayer, through the ministers of the Church, who are always at our disposal to guide and help and encourage, but however it comes, we may always be sure that it does come, according to our needs, and sufficien to enable us to overcome any temptation or difficult that may beset us. For, surely, God would not command us to do the impossible. God would not set us a task, and then deny us the strength to perform it. Nor would He, since His greatest desire is our sanctification, impose conditions too hard for

us to fulfill, or refuse to help us when we find the task too great to perform unaided.

Peroration: The responsibility, then, rests upon us. We know what God requires and desires of us. We know that He will assist us in every possible way to fulfill His will, if we honestly and earnestly set our wills in accord with His. But God, who created us without our will, will not save us without our will. We must do our part, and do it willingly, purposefully, actively. The first step is to make an act of the will, submitting ourselves entirely to God, resolving rather to die than to turn aside from His service. Then, we must make full use of the help God offers, keeping ourselves in the state of grace by constant and careful use of the means of grace. If we fall, we must lose no time in getting back to God's favor. If we succeed, we must give Him the glory, knowing that but for His help, we could do nothing of ourselves. Knowing, too, that if our wills are set towards holiness, as His will is set towards our sanctification, we must and will succeed in the greatest and most important business of life, the salvation of our souls.

Third Sunday in Lent

(Ephesians 5:3 and 4) But ... all uncleanness let it not so much as be named among you, ... nor obscenity, nor foolish talking, nor scurrility which is to no purpose.

No one knowing modern life, even in its most refined and cultured forms, can be blind to the fact that we live in an age marked by laxity of morals, decay of manners, and a freedom, or rather a boldness, of speech which was unknown, save in the lowest dregs of life, a few years ago. It may be claimed, perhaps, that the present generation is no worse than the last, but none can maintain that people today are not more outspoken about vice than their grandfathers were. Even aside from downright evil talk, matters are openly discussed nowadays which formerly it was considered, to say the least, impolite to mention. Unfortunately there has always been a good deal of "smutty talk," many bad books and plays, but never before has this sort of thing been so open and so widespread as today.

(1) Offenders against propriety (to say nothing of the Apostolic Command, contained in the Epistle just read) are not limited to any one class of people. Bad boys have, for generations, brought the blush of shame to decent people by chalking up unclean words on walls. But it has remained for the twentieth century to distinguish itself by bandying the scientific equivalents of such words in general conversation and in books. Men in their clubs and common market place have unfortunately, swapped dubious anecdotes from the time of paganism and probably before. But it is only now that these same stories,

elaborated into many chapters, could be procured in any book store, and read by our boys and girls openly and without reproof from parents, who also have read them. The e used to be some things which were never mentioned in the presence of ladies. today, it is the so-called "ladies" who joke and laugh about them, not only among themselves, but in general company.

(2) Innocence has ever been one of the rarest of fl wers. It might be asked if our boasted modern civilization has made it any less rare. If our children today preserve it, it is little short of a miracle, what with stories of vice and crime filling our newspapers, discussions of them on every lip, and vivid representations of them glowing on most movie screens and in many theatres. We need not blind our eyes to actual conditions. But do we need to talk of them so constantly and so freely? Serious discussion is, of course, legitimate, and to some purpose. It is the idle, vicious, purposeless talk that the Apostle condemns, and he condemns it because it is evidence of moral obliquity, and, even though it sometimes may not do any harm, it never does any good.

(3) "Out of the fullness of the heart, the mouth speaks." Clean-minded men and women do not use unclean language, men who are really gentlemen do not tell "smutty stories," women who are really modest do not retail unsavory scandals, young people who are honestly struggling to preserve their virtue do not place themselves in circumstances or take part in conversations which they certainly know are an occasion of sin. St. Paul, in the text cited, holds up a standard of gentility, for the laxness of speech which he condemns is not only sinful, but vulgar as well. True, vulgarity, in speech, in dress, in manners, is one of the strange developments of the social life of our time. But it cannot be said in terms too strong, that Catholics have no part nor lot in such things. For the Catholic Church, whether in conflict with the corruption of paganism, or the decadence of modern life, holds up an ideal of character in

which the virtue of holy purity is the most necessary element. We Catholics are taught, even before we know what the teaching means, to shun not only impurity in deed, but in thought and word as well.

Peroration: What a service we can do for the world, for society and for the Church, in making a more vigorous effo t towards living up to this high ideal. We may well make a beginning by guarding our speech, by refusing absolutely to permit our lips to offend God and man in this manner. True, words are superficial things, and a man may be uncouth of speech and at the same time pure in heart. He may be. But usually the foul-mouthed man is also a man of evil heart and mind. Self-control in the use of words will help to self-control in actions, nordare we forget the example we owe to the little ones, and more than the example, the positive precepts we should inculcate in their sensitive minds. It is far better to wash a child's mouth with soap the first time he brings in an obscene word from the street, than to snicker and laugh at his precocity, as all too many do. And if he must hear such things, let it not be from Catholics, not from parents, not from older brothers or sisters. Real blasphemy is rare. I leave it to your own experience to say just how common impurity in speech is in your own neighborhood.

For the honor of God, for the sake of the immaculate purity of Mary, for the sake of the good name of our Holy Mother the Church, let us have done with this filthiness of speech which is beyond doubt one of the crying evils of our time.

Fourth Sunday in Lent

(Galatians 4:31) By the freedom wherewith Christ hath made us free.

The e is a great deal of talk, in this day and generation of ours, about freedom, and most of it is very foolish talk, which demands not freedom, but license. For freedom, rightly understood, does not mean complete liberty from all restraint, utter disregard for all authority, nor the right of anyone to do as he pleases, regardless of the convenience and rights of others. When the heroine of the popular novel crys out: "I want to be free to live my own life," or when the young man of today leaves home because, as he says, "he wants to be his own master," it usually means that they really want not freedom, but liberty from the restraint, so that they may indulge themselves, plunge into all sorts of excesses, "sow their wild oats," in short, license if not licentiousness.

(1) In the early Church there was much discussion as to how far the Law of Moses was binding upon the consciences of Christians. The e never was any question, of course, about the Ten Commandments, for those enshrined and epitomized the principles of the moral law, the divine law, which in its very nature could never be abrogated or changed. But various ceremonial and sumptuary laws, and the great mass of customs and observances which had grown up in the generations of Jewish formalism, were a burden too great to be borne. The Council of Jerusalem, at which St. Peter himself presided, declared that these non-essential laws of the Jewish religion had been done

away, that the Catholic Church and Catholic people were not bound by them. Compared to this enormous mass of observances and regulations, the commandments of the Church are indeed a freedom which we are all too slow to appreciate. After all, it is not very much which our religion requires of us. And those laws that do bind us are very easily seen to be beneficial and advantageous.

(2) The e can be no liberty without law, for liberty does not mean that every man shall do as he pleases, regardless of everyone else. What confusion would inevitably result from such a conception of freedom! In our civic life we are free so long as we obey the law. Break the law, and our liberty is taken away. The law, then, insures liberty, under due and proper restraints, which are imposed in view of the good of the individual and of others whose rights must also be protected. A little study will convince a thoughtful man that the moral law, as taught by the Catholic Church, is divinely calculated to be for the greatest good of all. And so long as we obey it, we are free, free in conscience, free to enjoy life in the best and highest ways, free also from the dread of sin, which takes all joy out of this life and endangers, even when it does not rob us of, our happiness in the life to come.

(3) Too often we fail to appreciate all this. Too often we think of liberty and freedom as purely individual matters, as meaning nothing more than that we, as individuals, shall enjoy ourselves regardless of laws, reckless of consequences, selfishly unmindful of the rights of others. And, before we know it, we are slaves, tied and bound with the chain of our sins, our freedom taken away from us because we did not know how to use it properly. Look at the drunkard, the libertine, the miser. Are these men free, or are they slaves to their own hideous vices? They do as they please; and God lets them, because man's will is free, free that he may acquire merit by following the good and resisting the evil, free that he may obey the law, free in

order that he may serve the King of kings whose service alone is perfect freedom.

Peroration: It is, then, that we may serve God and obey His Commandments, voluntarily and of our own consent, that our wills are free. And when we make the wrong choice, doing evil instead of good, and thus bringing ourselves into the worst sort of slavery, the goodness and mercy of God offers us yet another opportunity to make the oblation of ourselves. By Penance, by sincere and perfect contrition, by the salutary absolution of the sacramental tribunal, Christ gives us back our freedom. And it is indeed true freedom that He brings to us, freedom of heart and mind and conscience, freedom from the guilt of sin, freedom from remorse, freedom from hell. Shall we, then, be so foolish, so headstrong as to return once more into the prison of sin? Think of all Jesus Christ has done for us, remanding the Old Law except in its fundamental precepts, all of them for our best good; giving us our free will in order that we may merit by becoming His willing servants; striking off from our hands the shackles of sin which we ourselves had forged; and last, but not least, summoning us to His obedience that we may crown Him King of our lives, and thus become truly free men.

Passion Sunday

(Hebrews 9:11) Christ being come, a high priest.

As the holy season of Lent draws towards its close, and we come closer and closer to Calvary, it is well to remind ourselves that, although the Church sets apart this portion of Lent for the contemplation of the Passion of Christ, and Good Friday for the special veneration of the Cross, we come to Calvary every day in the holy sacrifice of the Mass. The Mass is Calvary. We cannot fully understand either Calvary or the Mass apart each from the other. For in both the priest, the altar, the sacrifice, is the same

(1) Our blessed Lord and Saviour is called "the Great High Priest." In the Old Testament it was prophesied of Him that He should be "a priest forever, after the order of Melchizedech." As the High Priest of the human race He offers Himself upon the altar of the Cross as the one, perfect and sufficien Sacrifice for sin. Had He not been God, true God as well as true Man, His death could not have availed for the atonement for sin, His Blood could not have cleansed one single soul from its guilt before God. But, because He is God, His sacrifice is infinite, and can, by its application to our souls, remit the infinite guilt of sin. Because He is God, His sacrifice is eternal, as real today as it was when first it was offe ed on Calvary. So it is that we can plead that Holy Sacrifice in the Mass. We do not repeat it, we do not copy it, but we renew it and offer it each day af esh in the sight of God the Father.

(2) The earthly priests, by whose anointed hands the Holy Sacrifice is offe ed, are what they are because they have been

admitted to a share in the Eternal Priesthood of Christ. Their consecration, their commission, their powers, come directly from Christ, through the Catholic Church, and in no other way can any man claim to have divine authority to exercise the sacred ministry of the priesthood. This is the great diffence between the view that the Church takes of the priesthood, and the Protestant theory of the ministry as a representative function derived from a sect or a congregation. It is this that lifts the Catholic priest above men, above angels, the fact that he has been called by our Blessed Lord Himself and admitted into a share of His eternal sacerdotium. To him, Christ has delegated His own powers. Whatever the priest does, as a priest, he does as the representative of Christ, the alter Christus, so that what the priest does is really done by Christ Himself.

(3) It is thus that our Lord has chosen to continue His ministry in the world, down through the ages to the end of time. The functions of the Catholic priest carry on the work of Christ. The first and most important of these functions is to offer Sacrifice, as the first and most important work of Christ was to offer Himself upon the Cross as our Great High Priest. Christ also forgave sins, and gave to His priests the tremendous power of binding and loosing. Christ preached the truth, and through the Church He commissions His priests to do the same. How often was not the Hand of Christ raised in blessing, and the anointed hands of the priests of the Catholic Church are ceaselessly raised to impart that same blessing with the Sign of the Cross. It was not for nothing that Jesus said to the Apostles, who were the nucleus of the Catholic priesthood, "As the Father sent me, I also send you."

Peroration: A great Saint once gave this advice to the men and boys of his congregation: "If you should chance to meet in the street, an angel and a priest, salute the priest first!" Catholics are known everywhere for their veneration of, and loyalty to, their priests. It is something more than respect shown to a wise and good man. It is homage shown to Christ Himself, whose representative the priest is. What benefits have we not received from those consecrated hands, what words of wise council from those blessed lips! How often have your priests stood between your souls and hell! How often have they brought God down upon the altar and given Him to you in Holy Communion! They have power to bind your sins upon you, no less than to loose them—how seldom they exercise this stern prerogative, which yet may be their sad duty if you do not show the proper dispositions for absolution. Honor and love them, then, not only for what they are to you as men, but far more for what they are as the representatives of Christ, sharers in His eternal priesthood, guardians of His truth, God's ambassadors to you, your ambassadors to God.

Palm Sunday

(A short "Fervorino," which may be added to the announcements or at the end of the reading of the Passion in the Vernacular.)

The ceremonies of Holy Church on this day preach in action a most powerful sermon. They are so simple that a child can understand them, so ancient that they are indeed venerable, and yet so splendid that they may, and should, lift the hearts of all who witness them to the very throne of God itself.

The Blessing of the Palms, and the Procession recall most vividly the sacred events of this day, the entrance of Our Lord into the Holy City of Jerusalem in triumph, hailed by the multitude as their King. Yet almost at once the glad cries of welcome are changed to the hoarse shouts of the mob demanding that Christ should be crucified. So, in the ceremonies of the Church, hardly has the Mass begun, before the same voices that, so short a time before, had chanted Hosanna, must begin the sad melodies of "The Passion."

Thus we renew our memories of the events of this day, which is, to us, not merely a commemoration of happenings in a long-distant past, but a matter of vital and present importance in our life today. For we admit our part in all this, we admit that we, no less than those Jews of ancient times, are responsible for the sufferings and death of our dear Lord. By our sins we crucify Him afresh and put him to shame. Shall we not, on this Palm Sunday, beg him to put His passion and Cross between us and the due reward of our sins that we may not cease to hail him as our King in this life and in the life to come?

Easter

(1 Corinthians 5:7) Christ our Pasch is sacrificed, therefore let us feast.

For six long weeks the Catholic Church has been bowed in penitential sorrow, her altars draped in somber colors, her people afflictin themselves with fasting, busying themselves with prayer. Day by day the gloom has deepened, until, with Holy Week, it reached its crisis in the sad solemnities of the last three days, when the altars stood stripped and desolate, the bells hung silent, the black garb of death and mourning was thrown over all. Now, in a moment, all is suddenly changed. The bells ring out once more, as with all the pomp and splendor of our ancient rites we raise again the glad anthems of the Easter Alleluia, and hail our Saviour risen from the grave in triumph, a triumph in which we, even we, are called to share.

(1) Who would not be happy on such a glorious day! Who would not be thrilled by the wonderful message: Death is defeated, Sin is conquered, Man is freed from the age-long curse, Jesus lives! For this same Jesus, whom we followed in spirit to Calvary and to the tomb, is ours—our Lord, our Saviour, our eternal King. He is not a mere man who trod this earth two thousand years ago, speaking as never man spake, work-ing great miracles, undergoing great sufferings, and at last, by a stupendous miracle, coming back from the grave itself. We know that He did all this for us because He loves us, because He is our God, and because in this manner He willed to share our life, to come near to us, to mingle with us in our joys and sorrows, that He might draw us ever

closer to Himself. For, having lived and died and risen again, for us men and for our salvation, His one desire is that we may come into ever closer union with Him. Therefore He makes of Himself "our Pasch," and comes, our Risen, Glorious Christ, to meet us on this hap-py Easter morning, in the Blessed Sacrament.

(2) It is true, the Blessed Sacrament comes to us out of the very heart of the Passion of Christ. Instituted at the Last Supper, made availing by the death on Calvary (for the Mass, never forget it, is Calvary) the Blessed Sacrament, which is none other than Jesus Himself, Risen and Glorified, is indeed the triumph of His love for human souls. Under the Old Law, the Jews feasted on the flesh of the Paschal Lamb, which was but the type and symbol of Him who should be the Lamb of God. We, whose wonderful privilege it is to live under the Dispensation of the New Law, feast on the Living Flesh of Christ, our Pasch who was sacrificed for us, and who ever lives to make intercession for us. This miracle of grace is only possible because Jesus is God. Easter is the witness and the proof of that, for since the beginning of the world never was it known that a man raised himself by his own power from the dead. The Blessed Sacrament is also the witness and the proof of it, for never, among any people, was it known that for centuries upon centuries the worshippers of any hero, or human leader, however exalted or admirable, should worship his presence under such a form and in such a manner.

(3) Easter is possible only because Christ is God. Holy Communion is possible only because Christ is God. The fogiveness of sins is possible only because Christ is God. The Catholic Church is possible only because Christ is God. What a superb vindication of the claims of Jesus Christ this day is! For two thousand years it has been kept with untold rejoicing by countless happy souls, and kept through the ages in the same way. Always it has been the day of acclamation of the God-Man as victor over death. Always

it has been the day for receiving Him in Holy Communion. Always it has been the day for souls, washed from sin in the waters of Baptism, or by the application of the Precious Blood in the Sacrament of Penance, to renew their allegiance to their Risen King. Al-ways it has been the day of greatest pomp and rejoicing in the Catholic Church.

Peroration: The precept of the Paschal Communion binds us in conscience—but how much more in heart! For beyond our wonder at the stupendous miracle of the Resurrection, and the even more tremendous miracle of the Mass, must always be our love for Jesus Christ. As we mourned for His sufferings, and for our sins which caused them, out of love for Him; so should we rejoice in His triumph, and receive Him as our King, out of love for Him. He is our God, but He is our Friend, our Saviour, our Lover. Let us worship Him, obey Him, serve Him, but always because we love Him.

Low Sunday

(1 St. John 5:5) This is the victory that overcometh the world, our faith.

The history of the world since the first Easter Day has been but the story of the continual triumph of the Catholic Faith. And this in spite of opposition, persecutions from without, treachery within, set-backs of all sorts, against which no merely human system could have possibly been successful. The message of the Catholic Church was the last thing that anyone would have thought could convert the world. A religion of astounding mysteries, teaching that God had become Man, and so had died and risen again, and though returned to His Father's throne in Heaven was still in the world under the appearance of the most common of all material things, bread and wine. A religion that taught humility, and purity, and self-sacrifice. A moral code that ran contrary to the spirit of the age in which it was proclaimed and every age since. Yet, wherever that religion was preached, it made converts; converts who for centuries must face death for their new-found faith. Even when that age of persecutions was past, the Faith made demands on men no less urgent, yet men fulfilled them

(1) The world has never understood the power of the Faith. Men are today mystified by the strength of the Catholic religion, no less than Nero was amazed at the fortitude of the martyrs. Yet every Catholic child knows the secret—knows that Christ Himself is the strength of those who unite themselves to Him. For it is the faith of loving hearts in Christ which

gives them the victory. This Catholic Faith of ours is not merely a philosophical or theological system of human thought. It is that, to be sure, the most perfect intellectual system ever known among men; but it is vastly more than that. Millions who knew nothing of philosophy or of theology have died for the Faith, millions more, simple and unlearned as well as the greatest minds of the world, have lived by it. A few statements of belief, a few simple rules of conduct—could these, however divine their origin, give men such power? Yes, for they center around a Person, Jesus Christ, a living person, not a dead historical record.

(2) It is this fact that the Catholic Church believes in, worships and enshrines in her temples and in the hearts of her people, the Living, Present Christ, that has given her faith such power through the ages. But the Catholic Church, though she is a divine institution, is made up of individuals, and her faith is their Faith, by which they, too, may overcome the world. By the world we mean sin, and all its dreadful consequences,—unbelief, hardness of heart, and finally death itself. All that is at enmity with God and the souls of men. Only Faith can overcome in the battle against such foes as these. Look at the world, consider its temptations, its pride, its lust, its avarice, its mad pursuit of pleasure that it mistakes for happiness. Do you think you could save your soul, in spite of such opposition as that, without your Faith, with-out the help of your Religion, without the Sacraments of your Holy Mother the Catholic Church?

(3) Experience teaches us that we must fail unless we fight the good fight of Faith. We have tried to fight in our own strength, and we have always lost the battle. Men have devised their little systems of "self-help" and they have always been beaten. Some have tried to meet the world with a mutilated religion, a negative faith which knows not what it does believe, but is quite sure of what it does not believe. And the non-Catholic world today is freely admitting

the failure of what it calls "the churches" to give their members the strength to win the fight against sin, the world, and the devil. They fail because they have not the truth, because their beliefs are mistaken. We fail because, having the Faith, we do not practice it as we ought.

Peroration: But we can have our part in the triumph of the Faith. It can be, it should be, our triumph too. This glorious Easter season should teach us one great lesson—the lesson of Faith. How can we sufficientl appreciate the treasure we have in our Religion? How can we ever be thankful enough that we are Catholics? How can we show God our gratitude for all that our Faith tells us He has done, and will do, for us? Simply by practicing our Religion, simply by living good Catholic lives, simply by adding to our intellectual position as Catholics, the good works which our Faith demands. For it is not enough to believe only (do not the devils also believe and tremble) we must live our Faith, and in so doing we shall find that the victory is ours, not by our own might, but by the power and strength of the Faith that is ours by the mercy of God.

Second Sunday After Easter

(1 St. Peter 2:25) For you were as sheep going astray: but you are now converted to the Shepherd and Bishop of your souls.

Not the least of the consoling thoughts of Eastertide is the knowledge that at this joyful season countless souls have been reconciled to God in the reception of the Sacraments. At no other time are our tribunals and our altars so thronged. It is true, thank God, that most of our people frequent the Sacraments. Monthly and weekly, and even daily Communion, is, in our time, the rule rather than the exception. The proportion of Catholics who content themselves with the performance of "the Easter Duty" is comparatively small, and it is a source of great encouragement to our priests that their people evince so great a zeal in the performance of their religious duties throughout the year. But at Eastertide there are always some who come back after a long absence, they may be turned from a terrible life of sin, to make a fresh start in the great work of saving their souls, and these rejoice not only the hearts of our priests, but even more the Sacred Heart of Jesus.

(1) "To err is human, to forgive divine," so says the poet, and how true it is! Not only is our fallen nature prone to evil, but we are surrounded with all sorts of temptations to lead us away from the paths of justice. The story of most lives is the continued and repeated story of sin after sin, repentance after repentance. But, how thankful we should be that it is possible for us to be forgiven and to start all over again! How terrible is that false teaching (which some of our non-Catholic breth-

ren hold) that some are inevitably destined to perdition, while others, no matter what they do, cannot help but be saved! Our wills are free, and it is for us to choose the path we shall tread. We cannot be forced into sin without our consent, and even the grace of God cannot force us into repentance, for the same free will chooses evil under the influence of Satan, chooses to return to God under the influence of His tender attraction.

(2) We may, we must, resist temptation with all our strength; and aided by divine grace it is perfectly possible for us to keep ourselves free from serious sin all our life long. Unfortunately we do not always resist as manfully as we should, nor do we make full use of the graces which would assist us so powerfully did we only summon them to our aid in the battle of life. Even more unfortunately, we do not always yield to the promptings of grace as we should, but we put off our repentance, we dally with sin, we refuse to be reconciled with God. But like the Good Shepherd which He is, God will not let us wander along the ways of sin, but comes out after us, seeking that which is lost, calling us, begging us to return to the fold. Woe to us if we refuse to hear that kind and loving voice pleading in our hearts, for if we are obdurate the time will come when Jesus must say to us, not "Come unto Me," but "Depart from Me into eternal life."

(3) Our loving Saviour is always ready to receive us when we return to Him in penitence for our sins which have so grieved His Sacred Heart. But there are certain seasons of grace when He seems to call us more insistently, and Eastertide is one of these. It is not only our duty which commands us, under pain of ceasing to be practical Catholics, to approach the Sacraments of Penance and Holy Communion during the Paschal season: it also our high and holy privilege, our opportunity to turn from carelessness and indiffe ence, to begin a new life, to rise from the death of sin to the life of justice. If we have not heard the voice of Christ calling to us all through the year,

warning us of our danger, admonishing us of the punishments in store for those who persistently reject Him, appealing to us in so many diffe ent ways to turn to Him; now at least we dare not to be indiffe ent any longer. Why put off your Easter duty another day, if indeed, you have not already informed it? The longer you wait, the harder it will be. Do not, I beg of you, presume and impose upon the mercy of God another hour, but come back to your duty, begin your new life, and by the Grace of God be more devout and careful in the future.

Peroration: The law of the Church commands us that we receive the Sacraments at least once every year, during the Paschal Season. But what sort of a Christian, what sort of a Catholic, what sort of a lover of Jesus, will be content with that required minimum? When God is so generous with us, surrounding us with opportunities to partake His grace and favors, who would be so stingy with God, so cruel to his own soul, as to seek to content himself with mere fulfilling of the letter of the law? It is the mind of our Holy Mother the Church, so well expressed by that Pope of saintly memory, the late Pius X, that all Catholics should approach the Sacraments frequently. The most we can do is to receive Holy Communion daily: the least we can do is to perform our Easter duty. When, at your last hour, Jesus ceases to be to you the Good Shepherd and becomes your Eternal Judge, which sort of a Catholic would you rather have been?

Third Sunday After Easter

(St. James 1:21) For so is the will of God, that by well-doing you may put to silence the ignorance of foolish men.

"Actions speak louder than words." That is the way in which that old familiar proverb express the same thought as our text, and a very true, and very deep, and very important thought it is. For we live in a time when a great many people are saying a great many things against the Catholic Faith and the Catholic people, and in our annoyance we are very prone to "talk back" instead of taking the most effective means of stopping the mouths of our calumniators, the means mentioned in our text, the means God wishes us to take.

(1) It is manifestly unfair that any system, religious or otherwise, should be judged by those who fail to practice it. Yet such is human nature that men are ever ready to apply this false standard of judgement. They see a bad Catholic, who has not been to Mass for years, who lives a scandalous life, but who is, nevertheless known to be, nominally, a Catholic: and they say "if that is the Catholic religion, none of it for me!" Of course it is unfair, but it is a fact which must reckon with. Your Church is judged by you. For most non-Catholics know little or nothing about your Church, but your neighbors do know you, and they know you are Catholic. What more natural than that they should form their estimate of your Faith by your practice of it or your failure to practice it?

(2) Whether you like it or not, you are marked men and women in your neighborhood, your community. If for nothing

else, our habit of attending Church services at unusual hours would serve to distinguish us from our non-Catholic friends, to say nothing of our habit of carrying religious articles about with us, or having them in our homes. Now, if we are really good people, no one will remark about these things, but a bad man with beads in his pocket, or a bad woman with a medal round her neck, strikes anybody, Catholic or non-Catholic, as incongruous. Somehow or other, non-Catholics expect us to be diffe ent. They would not admit it, but they really expect us to be better. If we are not, they discredit the Church, when they ought to discredit us as individuals who fail to live up to the teachings of our religion.

(3) Most of the calumnies against the Catholic Church are founded on ignorance of historical facts or doctrinal formulas. But most of the prejudice against the Catholic Church is the fault of our own people failing to practice their religion and so giving a bad example to those outside the fold. We do not like to hear such facts, but they are true for all that. If all our people were consistent, practical Catholics, Living their religion day by day, the anti-Catholic campaign would die in six months, in spite of the vast sums of money being poured into it by those who hate the Church for what it is, and employ professionals to spread false ideas about it, making non-Catholics into anti-Catholics by willful misrepresentations.

Peroration: You cannot answer such attacks by argument alone, or by presentation of historical facts, or by the correction of flagrant misunderstanding. The Catholic answer to charges against the Church is seldom heard by those who hear the calumnies first. Many are prejudiced against the Church without reason, but because they are prejudiced, they are not open to reason for hating the Church, which seem to them reasonable. Upon investigation these personal animosities usually prove to be the result of a real or fancied wrong done by some individ-ual Catholic, who was not a good Catholic in any sense of the phrase. The great mass of our fellow-citizens are fair-minded, and if they see a good example given by Catholics they will discount the unsupported lies of professional agitators.

What a responsibility is thus laid upon us!

Fourth Sunday After Easter

(St. James 1:20) For the anger of man worketh not in the justice of God.

Anger, as we all know, is one of the seven deadly sins, and although (thank God) it is comparatively rare in its extreme forms, it is all too common in its lesser manifestations. Almost always it is the result of pride, the leader and root of all capital sins, and it is because our pride or vanity is wounded that we fla e up in ill temper, speak angry words, even go so far as strike or injure those who we fancy have not been sufficientl impressed with the importance of our views or wishes. Be it said to our credit, we are almost always sorry enough after one of these outburst, and try to excuse ourselves on the plea of "nerves," "a naturally quick temper," or "intolerable provocation." And it is perfectly true that patience is not a natural virtue in the sense that the average human being is endowed with it. But it is our duty to cultivate patience, and to overcome, by the grace of God, the impulses of our fallen nature towards anger, even in its lesser forms.

(1) The most common of these venial varieties of anger is impatience, with self and with others, which results in lit-tle momentary flare-ups, a sharp word, or, it may even be, a smouldering resentment which may gather strength if we do not repress and overcome it, till it bursts forth in a really serious sin. Our ordinary daily life furnishes innumerable occasions; the stupidity of others or our own; the disobedience of children or employees; the little slights put upon us by those with whom we come in

in contact; the failure of a cherished plan; all these, and many more, are temptations to us to relax that self-control which should characterize the Christian man or woman. Then there are more weighty occasions, real injuries, downright insults, injustices, calumnies, deep disappointments brought about through the fault of others, and these are calculated by the enemy of our souls to arouse the base passion of anger within us and to lead us to seek redress and revenge.

(2) But revenge is forbidden us by our Holy Religion. "Revenge not yourselves, my dearly beloved; but give place unto wrath, for it is written, Revenge is mine, I will repay, saith the Lord" (Romans 12:19, quoting Deuteronomy 32:35). The teaching of our Blessed Lord on this matter is plain and familiar to us all, with its promise of a blessing upon the meek. Most of all, the divine example of our Saviour, who prayed for His murderers, and was patient under unutterable insults, injustice, and suffering, shows us how unworthy is this desire, on the part of His followers, to "get even" for every slight and injury. Indeed, our own forgiveness is made to depend on our forgiveness of others (St. Matthew 6:15), and in the Lord's Prayer we acknowledge this condition. Yet how often in practice we ignore it, harboring resentment, refusing to forgive. Holding our anger in spite of the admonition, "Let not the sun go down upon your anger" (Ephesians 4:26).

(3) Irritability whatever may be its cause has a tendency to grow into a fi ed habit; a choleric disposition yields but hardly to the discipline of self-control. How easy it is for a man or woman to gain the reputation of being sharp-tongued, quick to anger, peevish, hard to get along with. And all these things are evidences of pride, lack of self-control, weakness of character. Uncontrolled anger is characteristic of children, as is also the retention of ill feelings even after the one who has injured us has sought to make reparation. How much of the profanity of our day arises from just such lack of self-control, while the

sad condition of so many of our homes may be traced to the unbridled and futile impatience of parents. Surely we have, all of us, great need to learn the long, slow lesson of patience.

Peroration: But patience, certainly is a gift of God, and can only be attained by the assistance of His grace. Do we practice patience, especially when tempted to its opposite? The old-fashioned maxim, "Count ten before you speak," is well enough in its way, but how much better to pray before we speak. The prayer to St. Michael the Archangel, said after Low Mass, and so familiar to us all, is an excellent prophylactic against sins of anger and impatience.

If mention has not been made here of the grave sins of anger; violence, murder, revengeful injury to the bodies or reputations or property of others, it is because if we diligently root out the lesser sins of this sort, we shall hardly be likely to fall before the rarer temptations which come only under extraordinary circumstances. Yet we should pray to be delivered from such trials, lest they prove too much for our weakness. Anyone is likely to be placed, some time during life, in a position where anything is possible. Next to the grace of God, a long training in self-control, a constant exercise of patience, is the best safe-guard against the upsurging of sudden passion of any sort, and especially of anger. But when we have done all in our power to discipline and restrain ourselves habitually, we are still human, still weak. Watch and pray, then, that you enter not into temptation (St. Mark 14:38).

Fifth Sunday After Easter

(St. James 1:22) Be ye doers of the word, and not hearers only, deceiving your own selves.

You have noticed, perhaps, in reading the Epistles for this Easter season, the insistence on "good works," the practical side of religion, which the Church sets before us in these excerpts from the letters of the Apostles. For Eastertide is not merely the commemoration of the historical fact of the Resurrection of our Lord from the dead, it is also the witness and the reminder that we, too, as His disciples, have risen from the death of sin and entered upon the new life of right living. If this were not so, the Easter feast could mean but little to us, as of a far-off divine event which we are bidden admire, but which had a little or nothing to do with us personally, which did not touch us vitally, and so made hardly any diffe ence in our daily way of living.

(1) Too many people have just this impersonal and indif-ferent view of the great fact of Religion, regarding it as something beautiful and good, but quite outside of themselves, something to be admired but not practiced, something, of course, to die in, but not something to live by. The Apostle warns us expressly against this view, telling us that it is not enough to enroll our names among the number of believers, not enough to be "among those present" when the eternal truths are preached; but we must, if all this is to do us any good at all, in this world or the next, practice what we hear preached, really take our part in the spiritual activities of religion, really be Catholics as well as have the name of such.

(2) How often we hear it said of this man or that woman: "Oh, yes, he or she is a Catholic, but he doesn't work at it!" There are those who would feel insulted if you called them "Protestants" or said that they were not Catholics. Yet do not live as if they were Catholics, and anyone not knowing them intimately would never guess that they were Catholics. Questioned as to their faith, they could pass a good examination as to their orthodoxy. Yet their belief does not show in their lives to any marked degree. They may be fairly regular about "hearing Mass" on Sundays, not so good on holy days that fall during the week. While for as the Sacraments—well, they conform to the minimum requirements, and go to Confession and Communion during Eastertide. Their children are baptized, perhaps they make their first Communion, perhaps not. Yet they are Catholics, "hearers of the word," but at best lukewarm and careless "doers."

(3) The worst of it is that they fool themselves, though they do not fool anybody else. Life runs along with them just about as it does with anyone else. They are, in the eyes of the world, fairly good people. Of course they "don't set up to be saints," and if they are great sinners, they manage at least to keep up respectable appearances. They see so many people worse off, religiously, than themselves that they begin to think all is well with them. They have the faith! But "the devils also believe," yet their faith does not save them. The Catholic Church has never taught the Faith alone will save a man. Something more is required than a more or less intelligent acceptance of the eternal truths. Those truths must be put into practice, if they are to be to us anything more than interesting and beautiful abstractions. The question of the really honest and earnest Christian is "what must I do to be saved?" The honest and earnest Catholic is literally up and doing and not fooling himself with the thought that everything is all right so long as he is nominally a Catholic, and so within the ark of safety.

Peroration: It is now sufficientl long after Easter for us to cast up our spiritual accounts again. We received the Sacraments, it is to be hoped, on Easter day. We made, it is to be hoped, good resolutions; some effo t to change the way of our life, to overcome evil habits, to quit dangerous company and occasions of sin. Well, that was over a month ago—where do we stand now? Have we really "risen with Christ" to newness of life, or are we deceiving ourselves again, playing with the hell-fi e of sin, lapsing back into our old indiffe ence? We have heard, over and over again, what we ought to do, how it is possible for us to reform our lives so that they may really be worth living. Are we doing it? Has Lent and Easter meant anything to us, and if not, why not? Whose fault will it be if this glorious Eastertide shall pass and find us no better than we were before? God help us all to put into practice the words we hear, to be real Catholics, not deceiving and defrauding ourselves of the happiness that should be ours in the service of God.

Sunday in the Octave of the Ascension

(1 St. Peter 4:10) As every man has received grace, ministering the same one to another: as good stewards of the manifold grace of God.

We are accustomed, and quite rightly, to think of the priest of the Catholic Church as the ministers of divine grace, the stewards of mysteries of God. Yet there is a sense in which all Catholic people, as being the recipients of grace, are also its ministers in behalf of others. Our non-Catholic friends talk much of "the priesthood of the laity," and some of them have carried the idea to such an extent that they deny any special and sacramental priesthood at all. But there are many passages in the New Testament which show us that we are, all of us, in a sense, ministers, though not, of course, by virtue of ordination or as having any special authority and power. How, then, are lay people to minister the grace of God one to another, and so make more use of the treasures they receive than if they merely use them for themselves? For it is evident that we must not be selfish in our Religion. If God grants us favors, we are bound to share them with others, so far as we possibly can.

(1) We do this first of all by giving a good example to those, both Catholics and non- Catholics, with whom we come in daily contact. You cannot give a good example unless you are really good, and you cannot be really good without the grace of God. People easily see through pretended goodness, and judge us not merely by our profession, but by our performance. The inconsistent, careless Catholic is a positive harm both to

those of the household of Faith and those without. But without speaking one word, a good Catholic influences the lives of others, stirs the good to greater zeal, reproaches the bad, encourages those who are struggling after goodness by showing them that it is possible, by God's grace, for ordinary people to achieve solid virtue. What is this but a ministering of the grace of God, which you yourself have received, to others?

(2) We are taught in the Catechism that we receive the grace of God not only in and through the Sacraments, but also by prayer. Nor do we need to read the Lives of the Saints to learn of many instances of the good done to others by the fervent prayers of practical Catholics. Many a careless son or daughter has been won back to God and Religion by the prayers of a sorrowing mother, even as St. Monica gained the conversion of her son, afterwards St. Augustine. "The son of so many tears cannot be lost." Again and again converts to the Faith have ascribed their conversion to the prayers of their Catholic friends. Yet, how selfish most of us are with our prayers, like the old man who asked God to bless himself and his wife, his son John and his wife, "us four and no more!" Isn't that practically our attitude when we limit our petitions to the needs of a narrow circle, and even sometimes forget to mention those who may actually have asked us to pray for them? It is noticeable that those who have, as we say, "the gift of prayer," are very generous in their intercessions, including many souls in their petitions. And it is this generosity in ministering the grace of prayer which the Catholic Church encourages when she bids her children pray "for the Pope's intentions."

(3) The gift of Faith is one of the greatest graces of all, yet it almost seems as if it were the one which we are least willing to share with others. Yet every Catholic, good and bad alike, has constant opportunities to say a word in favor of the Faith to those outside the fold. Somehow our Catholic people are very timid about talking religion with non-Catholics. Sometimes

it is a sort of shame because they feel they are not sufficientl good Catholics to be able to discuss such sacred subjects with those who inquire about them. Yet we can hardly be called "stewards" of the grace of God if we do not seek to share this great grace with those who have it not. It may be that some non-Catholic friend is just waiting for a little encouragement from you. What a wonderful thing it would be if every Catholic should, by the help of God, make one convert each year!

Peroration: Sacramental grace is, of course, entrusted to the priests of the Catholic Church, to be by them administered and dispensed to the Faithful. But every one of you is, in a lesser though very real sense, in a position to pass on, to someone else who may need it more than yourself, some portion of the grace of God which has been given so generously to you. By good example, by prayer, by the spoken word, we can bring God's grace to those within and without the Fold. And we shall have to answer for it to God if we fail to realize this great responsibility.

Pentecost

(Acts 2:11) We have heard them speak in our own tongues the wonderful works of God.

This is one of the few Sundays of the year on which there is substituted for the Epistle a passage of scripture from some other part of the Bible. today, as befits the Feast of Pentecost, it is the account, from the Acts of the Apostles, of the coming of the Holy Ghost. This day is sometimes called "the birthday of the Catholic Church," and it is interesting to observe how thus, at the very beginning, the international and supra-racial character of the Church is declared. The Jewish Church, which was, until the day of Pentecost, the true Church of God on earth, was limited to one race and nation of people. Outsiders, Gentiles, could only enter it by changing not only their religion, but their nationality as well. But the Church which Christ founded, and which, on this day, became the dwelling-place of the Holy Ghost, was intended to go beyond the limits of nationality, to be indeed Catholic, Universal.

(1) Christ commanded His Apostles to go "teach all nations," which meant, of course, that the Church was to be world-wide in its scope. The various nationalities mentioned in the passage from the Book of the Acts, were represented by Jews, who were, then as now, scattered over all the world, Naturally, the first Christians were Jewish converts. But it was not long before the Gentiles began to throng into the Church, and those who thought that Christianity was to be but a Jewish sect, began to realize that "all men everywhere," every nation

and language, were to claim the name Catholic as their proud international title.

(2) It is important that we grasp the meaning of all this, because it is a fact of history that no other religious organization that the world has ever known could claim this universal char-acter. The old pagan religions were, like the Jewish faith, limited to particular races or nations. And it must be noted that the new religions, which sprang up from the time of the so-called Reformation in the sixteenth century, have all of them been racial or national, and no one of them has ever converted a nation to Christianity, as the Catholic Church did in the an-cient times. Lutheranism, for example, has been limited to the German people, or those descended from them. Anglicanism has been the peculiarity of English people, and those speaking that language. These, and other non-Catholic denominations, have made attempts to convert other peoples to their religion, but have never been successful in doing so. But the Catholic Church, imbued as it was with the Holy Ghost, went forth and made converts in every nation, every race, having a universal appeal which is as strong today as it was in the beginning.

(3) Humanly speaking, this has been possible because, while adapting itself to the national characteristics of various peoples, and preaching the Gospel to them in their own tongue, the Catholic Church has yet preserved a marvelous unity of doctrine and practice, and has, almost entirely, adhered to the use of the Latin tongue in its official acts and ceremonies. But the spread of the Church into every part of the world cannot be accounted for by human reasons. It is a miracle in itself, accomplished by supernatural means. Only a divine institution, vitalized and protected and guided by the Holy Ghost, could have such a power of attracting and satisfying people of such diverse attributes, needs, and customs. As on the day of Pente-cost, the Church has always had a message for all of them, in a language they could understand. And it is so today.

Peroration: Have you ever thought what a strange and wonderful thing it is that the Catholic Church is the spiritual home of such varied types of people;—not merely of diffe ent nationalities, but of widely diffe ent temperaments, of every shade of culture, rich and poor, learned and unlearned? She has never been the Church of a class, though, thank God, she has always been the Church of the poor. But kings have been proud to receive their crowns at her hands. The greatest scholars that the world has ever known have been her most loyal children. She has completely satisfied the rude barbarian and the most highly civilized peoples; indeed it is she who has transformed the ancient world of barbarism into the modern of civilization, and has done this simply as a side issue while accomplishing her great spiritual work for souls. It is indeed a proud heritage to be a Catholic. Truly the day of Pentecost is the birthday of the Church, and the beginning of her great and universal work, in which we also have our part.

Feast of the Most Holy Trinity

(Romans 11:36) For of Him, and by Him, and in Him are all things: to Him be glory forever. Amen.

The deepest and most impenetrable mystery of our holy Religion is that which teaches us that God is Thee Divine Persons, the Father, the Son, and the Holy Ghost, yet One God. The unaided reason could never have deduced this fact, although it could arrive at the truth of the existence of God, and could dimly discern His attributes. But it was left to divine revelation to declare this mystery of the Most Holy Trinity, beginning where reason leaves off, yet in no way contrary to reason. Once revealed, we must accept it, believing where we may not understand.

(1) Belief in God is inherent in human nature. There never was a nation, or tribe, of men, however debased by paganism, which did not cling to the idea of the supernatural, which did not believe in, and worship, God. The more highly civilized a people were, the closer did their beliefs come to the true faith in the One All-Holy God, Who in olden times revealed Himself to one chosen nation, the Jews. Amid the multiplicity of gods and goddesses of the ancient paganism, there were always elect souls who discerned the truth, for, as St. Paul says, God never left Himself without witnesses. But revelation is progressive: to the Jews God gave the knowledge that He was One, yet the Old Testament Scriptures are not lacking in indications of the fuller revelation for which God was preparing the world.

(2) When the Second Person of the Ever-Adorable Trinity became Incarnate, the world had, in the Person of Jesus Christ, the most complete revelation of God which it was possible for men to receive. Yet, at first, even His Disciples did not understand what He was trying to impress upon them. That is, that He was God. It was left for St. Peter, the Prince of the Apostles, to be the first of all men to declare the faith in the unique and everlasting Sonship of Christ. "Thou art the Christ, the Son of the Living God." It is idle for modern non-Catholics to claim that Jesus did not teach men that He was God, for so well did He impress his claim upon the minds of the people of His time that they put Him to death on the charge of blasphemy. Surely, if Jesus was not God, He was the greatest impostor the world has ever known. If He was not God, His character, instead of being what even non-Christians admit, the exemplification of the most perfect human goodness that ever was known, was nothing more nor less than a sham and a deception. Belief in the true Divinity of Christ is an integral part of the Religion which He founded. True God, and True Man, or else worse than nothing at all.

(3) According to His promise, our Divine Redeemer sent, on the Day of Pentecost, the Holy Ghost upon His Apostles, and thus into the Catholic Church. It was to be the particular work of the Thi d Person of the Most Holy Trinity to guide and protect the Church, making it impossible that she should ever teach as true that which is false. The history of the Catholic Church is inexplicable without this face; it is the secret of her continued life in a world which has, for centuries upon centuries, sought of her supernatural influenc upon the lives of men, of every nation and of widely different t ypes a nd needs. No merely human organization could have survived as she has survived; or could have accomplished the great work for countless souls which she has accomplished. History is the proof of this, for the man-made churches have shown

themselves incapable of doing the things which she has done, and still does.

Peroration: It is our great and marvelous privilege to profess the true Faith, to acknowledge the glory of the eternal Trinity, and in the power of the Divine Majesty to worship the unity (paraphrase of the Oration for the Feast). For we are creatures, children, of Our Father who is in Heaven; we have been re-deemed from sin and eternal death by the Incarnate Son; and we are living in the supernatural state of grace which is made possible for us by the ministrations of the Catholic Church which is indwelt by the Holy Ghost. We proclaim our Faith every time we "bless ourselves" with the Sign of the Cross. But we must do more than "profess" the Faith, we must practice it, live it, be a credit to it. For if, having the knowledge of the true Faith, we fail to live as becomes Catholics, so much the greater will be our retribution.

Sunday in the Octave of Corpus Christi

From the Epistle for the Feast. (1 Corinthians 11:26) For as often as you shall eat this bread, and drink the chalice, you shall show the death of the Lord, until He come.

Amid the sadness and gloom of Holy Week, under the very shadow of the Cross, Holy Church celebrated the institution of the Holy Eucharist. And now that Eastertide has been joyfully observed, Ascension day triumphantly commemorated, Pentecost greeted with great reverence, and the Feast of the Most Holy Trinity kept, she turns once more to the Eucharistic Christ, and bids us lift up our hearts in loving adoration to our Lord, enthroned upon our altars, in the Blessed Sacrament. Yet, in all our surpassing happiness, we are not permitted to forget that Holy Mass is Calvary, that the Christ of the Host is the Saving Victim slain for our sins, and as often as we eat this Bread and drink the Chalice, we show the death of the Lord.

(1) Without Calvary there would be no Mass; without the Cross there would be no Eucharist; had not Christ died, and risen again from the dead, we would not have the transcendent happiness of receiving Him in Holy Communion. It is the Risen and Glorified Body of Jesus which we receive in the Blessed Sacrament, but it is the same Body that hung on the Cross, wounded in hands and feet and side, the same Precious Blood which there fl wed forth to cleanse the whole world in its miraculous tide. So every Mass, every Communion, is a commemoration of the death of our Redeemer. But it is not merely a commemoration. Holy Mass is not a bare memorial service

(as non-Catholics regard their Communion Service), but it is, so to speak, the continuation of Calvary, Calvary every day.

(2) Holy Mass is a true sacrifice, having priest, altar and Victim. Jesus is the Great High Priest, who offers Himself as the spotless Victim, in this unbloody Sacrifice. This He does at the hands and by the ministrations of the priests of the Catholic Church, to whom He has given a share in His eternal priesthood, empowering and commissioning them to perform this service. It is the center of our worship, because Christ so ordered it, because Christ Himself is thereby brought to us, and we to Him. No merely human ceremony could ever take the place of Holy Mass—it is the one great official d otion of the Church, the only one which the faithful are obliged to attend.

(3) Those outside the Church find it hard to understand our ceremonies, our devotion, our loyalty and love for what seem to them but empty forms. But once the truth of the Real Presence of Christ in the Blessed Sacrament is grasped, all becomes plain, and is seen to be most fitting and proper. We make our churches as grand and as beautiful as our means permit, because they are the dwelling place of Jesus, who is God. We cheerfully obey the summons of Holy Church to gather Sunday by Sunday, because we come to worship Christ, truly present to receive our worship, to listen to our petitions, and to load us with favors. We engage in various ceremonies, because we wish to offer Him the worship of our whole being, and a worship in which the body did not share would be as imperfect as a worship into which we entered thoughtlessly and without the devotion of our hearts. We honor and love our priests, because it is they who bring Christ to us in this Holy Sacrament; who prepare our souls to receive Him by imparting His forgiveness of our sins; who teach us the blessed truths of the Religion which He founded.

Peroration: Our joy in our Eucharistic Lord finds full expression on this great feast day. But Jesus is with us all the days, according to His promise. We must not neglect Him at those times when He lays no obligation upon us to assist at Mass or to receive Holy Communion. The law of the Church, requiring us to assist at Mass on all Sundays of the year and on certain holy days, and to receive Holy Communion during the Easter season, is the minimum without which we cannot count ourselves as Catholics at all. But the Church has always urged her children not to content themselves with the formal fulfillment of the letter of the law. She has always invited and encouraged them to attend Mass and receive Holy Communion frequently. Her pious societies all have rules which recommend frequent Communion, monthly at least. And the saintly Pontiff, Pius X, has set forth the maximum privilege in exhorting as many as possible to receive Holy Communion daily. When our Lord is so generous with us, should we be so grudging and stingy with Him? When He calls us so lovingly to come to Him often, should we hold back?

Third Sunday After Pentecost

(1 St. Peter 5:8) Be sober and watch; because your adversary the devil, as a roaring lion, goeth about seeking whom he may devour.

At the beginning of the summer holiday season it is well that we remind ourselves of some of the special dangers against which it behooves us to be on our guard during the next few months. We are bound, at all times, to be watchful against temptation. Our Lord warned the Apostles: "Watch ye, and pray that ye enter not into temptation" (St. Matthew 26:41), and St. Mark tells us that He added the words, "And what I say to you, I say to all: Watch." (St. Mark 13:37) Though this is our duty always, it is especially so at times and season when, by past experience, we know that we are likely to be especially subjected to attacks from the evil one. To be forewarned is to be forearmed!

(1) The Catholic Religion is not a matter of seasons, but of our whole life, and its obligations bind us in conscience no less in summer than at any other time. Yet, human nature being what it is, we are all of us likely to become a bit slack sometimes, and certainly the temptation to neglect our religious duties is specially strong during the summer months, when both the weather and the now universal practice of vacation-taking (which includes Sunday trips and visits) conspire to make the fulfillment of our duties as practical Catholics less easy than at other times. But we may not excuse ourselves from our obligations lightly. We are bound to assist at Holy Mass on every Sunday and holy-day of obligation during the entire year. To

do this in summertime may mean a little self-denial, but certainly we owe this to God, who does so much for us. A practical point may be mentioned here; it is always better to make sure of hearing Mass before starting off for a trip, by auto or otherwise, rather than to take a chance on finding a church with Mass at a convenient hour, either along the road or at your destination.

(2) Of the many special temptations which arise to trouble us at this time of year we need not speak in detail. Suffic it to say that, while custom permits some relaxation of dignity, there can be and must be no vacation from decorum and propriety. Because the dress of women is lighter in summer than in winter, is no reason why it should be less modest. The men somehow find it possible to endure the warm weather without entirely undressing! If we live out-of-doors so much during these months, it is no reason why we should forget either manners or morality. Amusement and recreation are quite right if kept within proper bounds, but work cannot honestly be neglected at this season any more than at another, and the line must be strictly drawn between innocent amusements and pastimes which may quite easily become occasions of sin. Never was the admonition of the Apostles, quoted in our text, more needed than today, when a "good time" has somehow come to mean "a bad time" to all too many.

(3) The safeguard against temptation and sin is the same in summer as in winter. It is (need you be reminded?) the frequent reception of the Holy Sacraments. It is a grief to every priest to note how, as soon as school closes for the summer vacation, the attendance at week-day Mass falls off. It is hoped that this summer the children, especially, will make an effo t to attend Holy Mass often between Sundays. If you, older persons, are not accustomed to going to Mass during the week, or receiving Holy Communion frequently, there could be no better time to begin that pious practice, for most of us find it easier to get

up early during the summer, and in the cool of the morning it should be no great hardship to spend a half hour before God's altar, thus filling the soul with the graces so necessary to sanctify the rest of the day.

Peroration: The devil will take no vacation this summer! He is always alert and vigorous, and watching, watching for us to give him opportunities, watching for us to relax our vigilance, watching for us to grow slack and careless. And if he sees us taking a spiritual vacation, it will be indeed a fine chance for him to capture our souls and lead them into sin. The Church is no kill-joy. She is a kind Mother, who loves to see her children happy, enjoying themselves innocently and heartily. She knows that only the good can be truly happy. She knows that much which we call happiness is not really happiness at all, but hurtful alike to body and soul.

Make good resolutions for this coming summer, and by God's grace carry them out, and you will be able to look back upon it as the happiest summer of your life.

Fourth Sunday After Pentecost

(Romans 8:18) Brethren, the sufferings of this time are not worthy to be compared to the glory to come, that shall be revealed in us.

Perhaps the most perplexing riddle of this mortal life of ours is the mystery of suffering. It is easy enough to see why sinners should suffer, for toil, pain, disease and death are part of the curse of God upon sin. These evils entered the world with the Fall of our First Parents, and they are part of the temporal punishment for sin. But why good people should suffe , why innocent children should have to endure these chastisements, can only be understood in the light of God's mercy, for suffering, strange as it may seem, is a manifestation of the mercy of God no less than of His justice.

(1) The enormity of the malice of sin lies in the fact that it is an offence against God, who is infinite; the disobedience of a mere creature, against the known will of his Creator. The effects of sin in the soul are so terrible that we are accustomed to say that it kills the soul, not, of course, as regards its immortality, but with respect to supernatural, sanctifying grace. Not only does mortal sin actually cut the soul off from God, but it entails a punishment that is both temporal and eternal; in this life suffering for the body, which deliberately commits the sinful thought, word, or act; and, unless repentance shall bring us back to God's grace, eternal separation from God, the punishments of Hell, in the life to come.

(2) But even in His just wrath God remembers mercy. To our First Parents, in Eden, He promised the Saviour, who by

His all-sufficien death was to redeem the souls of men from the eternal consequences of their sins. By the Sacraments the Precious Blood of Jesus Christ is applied to our souls in pardon; in Baptism the stain of original sin is washed away, in Penance our actual sins are forgiven. So there remains only the temporal punishment for sin to be endured, first the disabilities and sufferings which are laid upon the whole race as the consequences of original sin, and then the direct consequences in this life of the sins we ourselves actually commit. It is part of the mercy of God that by enduring suffering in this world we may placate the justice of God, who permits us to expiate in this way while we live, that He may spare us in the next world.

(3) This expiation for sin, which we undertake in union with the sufferings of Christ, is not merely a passive endurance of what cannot be helped. As sin is the result of an evil choice by our will, rebelling against the known will of God, so the acquirement of merit, either by the performance of good works, or the patient endurance of sufferings which are part of the punishment due for sin, must be a matter of the will, which is now subjected to the will of God, accepting whatever He sends, or permits, in a spirit of penitence. God who made us without our consent, will not save us without our coöperation. As we sin voluntarily, so we must atone voluntarily, so far as lies in our power, for our sins, working out our salvation (as St. Paul puts it) in trembling and fear (Philippians 2:12). For suffering and pain are not blind and aimless forces to mar and spoil life. "We know that to them that love God all things work together unto good." (Romans 8:28).

Peroration: God wills us to be saved, God wills us to win Heaven at the last, God has prepared for us an eternity of happiness far exceeding any joy we can know in this world. But sin, and its consequences, stand between us and Heaven. Both sin and its consequences must be done away with, and that in a supernatural manner, before we can enter into the rest and bliss of Heaven. Christ, by His Passion, has made it possible for us to be rid of the eternal consequence of sin through sincere repentance and worthy reception of the Sacrament of Penance. By His favor also we may also expiate, even in this life, such a portion of the temporal punishment due to sin as to make our detention in Purgatory comparatively short. Cleansed we must be, from every last stain of even venial sin, before we can enter into Heaven. By good works, by the acceptance of suffering, we may, through the mercy of God, make atonement for our sins here and now. What a light this wonderful truth throws on the mystery of suffering! God permits us to suffer here that He may spare us hereafter. God allows even innocent children to endure pain that their crowns may be all the brighter in Heaven. Shall we not, then, accept whatever suffering life may bring us, in the spirit of penitence and with a contrite heart, offering it all up, through the Sacred Heart of Jesus, in expiation for our sins; looking forward to that blessed time when in Heaven we shall look back upon the toils and trials and pains of this life as a cheap price to pay for the glory of the Beatific Vision.

Fifth Sunday After Pentecost

(1 St. Peter 3:10) For he that will love life, and see good days, let him refrain his tongue from evil, and lips that they speak no guile (Ps. 33:13 quoted).

St. James tells us in his Epistle that "if any man offend not in word, the same is a perfect man" (St. James 3:2). And our Blessed Lord Himself warns us "that every idle word that men shall speak, they shall render an account of it in the day of judgement. For by thy words thou shalt be justified, and by thy words thou shalt be condemned" (St. Matthew 12:36, 3 7). We ought to realize, then how extremely important this matter of speech is, how easily and seriously we can sin through speech, what endless consequences even our careless words may have for our souls and the souls of others.

(1) All sin originates in the will, which, by giving consent to the temptations, turns away from the known will of God and contemplates evil with complaisance. We may not proceed to the wrong action, but by giving the assent of our wills we have disobeyed God, for He requires the union of our human wills with His divine will, the perfect obedience to His commandments which precludes even interior rebellion. Usually the course of sin, once consented to, is through speech into action. First we think of evil, and mentally consent to it. Then we speak to it, then we do it. But there are some sins which are complete in the mind, others which are done when the evil word is spoken, so we need not think that because we avoid what we are wont to call "sinful actions" we are therefore guiltless in the sight of God.

(2) St. Peter mentions, in today's lesson, the general sin of evil speaking, and the particular sin of guile or untruthfulness. It would be easy to classify sins of speech, blasphemy, false swearing, irreverent use of the Holy Name of God, rash and angry words, impure and suggestive talk, lying gossip, scandalous talk about others, unkind though perhaps true remarks about those whom we dislike—so one might go on through the long list of sins, some of them mortal, which are committed by unbridled and careless tongues. But we are to consider today more particularly the speaking of guile, untruthfulness.

(3) Without going into intricate discussions of the various kinds of lies, which are serious and which less culpable, we all know that lying is wrong. Usually it is a sign of either pride or cowardice. For we lie about ourselves and our achievements, making ourselves out to be much more clever and important persons than we really are, boasting unduly of what we have accomplished, "talking big," and this is through vanity, which, after all, is a weak sort of pride. Or, we find ourselves in a position, through our own fault or that of others, from which we seek to extricate ourselves by lying, rather than face the consequences bravely, and acknowledge ourselves to be in the wrong. "I didn't do it," it is the usual childish form of this lie, and it always requires (as, indeed, do most lies) another lie to cover up the first, and another to explain this, and so on, till we have forged a chain of deception which, unless we are exceptionally clever, will be our undoing sooner or later. Thus we see how foolish lying is, for of all sins it is perhaps the surest to find us out. Very few people have brains enough to be consistent and undetectable liars!

Peroration: The reputation for honesty is one of a man's most precious possessions. "His word is as good as his bond," is an enviable encomium for anyone. "You can't believe a word she says," may not be a just estimate of a person's general truthfulness, but it is a certain punishment for those who are not careful of the truth. Exaggeration, craftiness, boastfulness, equivocation, these sins bring a certain temporal punishment of their own in the loss of that proper human respect which we should all of us value, since it is at once a recognition of integ-rity and a check upon all our actions.

One of the calumnies frequently brought against the Catholic Church is that she permits her subjects to lie, and does not call untruthfulness a sin. Of course, we know that this is not so, but the very fact that this charge is falsely brought against us, should make us all the more careful to be strictly truthful and honest in all our words and dealings. Our text is something more than a restatement of the old proverb, "Honesty is the best policy." It is an assurance that truthfulness is a virtue which is not only its own reward, but for which God will reward us even here and now, in this life as well as in the life to come.

Sixth Sunday After Pentecost

(Romans 6:11) So do you also reckon that you are dead indeed to sin, but alive unto God, in Christ Jesus our Lord.

The e is a catch-phrase of the day which is heard all too often, especially on the lips of our young people, "I want to live my own life." We all know what it means—we want to be free to have our own way, to enjoy ourselves, even if it means sin, and we restive under the control of law, whether it be the law of God or of man, when it interferes with our convenience or our pleasure. But there is a deep fallacy in the phrase, and a very dangerous mistake in the thought that lies back of it. For we are in danger of forgetting what life is for, what its aim is, why it has been given to us, what we are to do with it. When we speak of living our own life, of doing what we please with it, we forget that life does not belong to us of our own right, but that it has been given or rather loaned, to us for a very definite purpose, which is to serve God and thus save our immortal souls.

(1) Reason alone would tell us that, since we are brought into this world without any action on our own part, without being consulted, the great gift of life cannot be ours unconditionally, to do with as we please. Religion teaches us that we are responsible to God for the use we make of our life, how we exercise our faculties and powers, and even human law makes us answerable for our actions to others besides ourselves. As a matter of practical fact, we know that while we are free to do as we please, we must be ready to face the consequences of what we do. But to suppose that, because we find ourselves in this world, endowed with certain capacities and

talents, we are therefore at liberty to throw life away carelessly, or squander it upon selfish enjoyment, is a foolish thought, —all religious teaching aside. Common sense tells us better. Human law warns us that we dare not "live our own life" if in so doing we interfere with the rights of others.

(2) But our Religion gives us a better reason than these for following the path of virtue and living our life in such a way that nothing we do will interfere with its chief end and aim. "you are not your own—for you are bought with a great price," says St. Paul (1 Corinthians 6:19-20). And he adds: "Glorify and bear God in your body." Which is a very pertinent remark in this connection, because when we hear people talking about "living their own life," we know perfectly well that they usually mean! Our bodies are certainly not our own to do with as we please. They are the temples of the Holy Ghost, the shrines of supernatural life, blessed by our Holy Mother the Church, intended not to drag down the soul to eternal loss, but to further it in its quest for everlasting life.

(3) The most serious sins which we commit are practically the theft of life for our own selfish enjoyment, the use of powers and faculties of body or mind in other ways than those in which God permits them to be used. None of us is perfect. "For all have sinned, and do need the glory of God" (Romans 3:23). It might, with considerable truth, be said that we have all had our fling, have given ourselves to sin, in one way or another. Yet God, in His infinite goodness, has set us free from sin, has forgiven us, restored us to His grace. Yet, somehow, we cling to the thought of life as an opportunity for pleasure, for our own aggrandizement, for anything and everything except its real purpose, which is to prepare our souls for Heaven. What folly! What madness! As if this life were all; as if there were to be no endless hereafter in which, indeed we shall live our own life, eternally determined by our own will here and now.

Peroration: Well, we may have sinned for a season, we may have forgotten our responsibility to God and our eternal destiny, but that is all past and gone. What of the future? The e is still time to accomplish the real business of life. St. Paul tells us how to do this, how to retrieve the past, how to assure the future. Count yourselves, he says, as already dead so far as sin is concerned, think of your life as belonging, not to yourself, but to God. This does not mean that all the joy will be taken out of life, for there is no happiness like the happiness of goodness. All that you will lose will be the doubtful pleasures of sin, which you have tasted and found nothing but trouble and disappointment. Surely experience should have taught us the folly of expecting to find happiness in disobedience to God's law. Very well, then, let us try the other way,—God's way. From this very moment begins a new life. We have done with sin, we are through with "living our own life" insofar as it conflicts with God's will for us.

Seventh Sunday After Pentecost

(Romans 6:23) For the wages of sin is death. But the grace of God, life everlasting.

Sin is disobedience to the known will of God. Because God is infinite, and sin is direct insult and injury to Him, its guilt is infinite, and its punishment terrible. Reason and common sense tell us this, there is no need of a revelation from Heaven to teach us so plain a truth. And our every-day experience tells us the same thing: we cannot transgress the laws of God, of nature, or of society, and expect to go scatheless, unpunished, or even undetected. Yet, though we know, or ought to know, this quite well, as a matter of fact we act as if this inexorable law of responsibility for our actions, this sure retribution for evil, were only a theory, without any practical application to ourselves.

(1) The e is a spirit abroad in the world today which whispers that anything is all right as long as you can, in the pregnant phrase of times, "get away with it." Being found out is the capital sin of worldling, and too many people guide their lives by the utterly false and wicked principle that so long as wrong-doing does not become known, so long as disgrace does not follow evil action, sin may be indulged in with impunity. Well, perhaps it sometimes can be, so far as this world is concerned. And if this world were all, we might indeed make reputation the sole arbiter of morality. But even in the world and among worldlings, the strange fact stands true that "murder will out," which is only the proverbial way of phrasing the Scriptural truth, "Know ye, that your sin shall overtake you"

(Numbers 32:23), or, in the words of our Blessed Lord Himself, "Nothing is covered which shall not be revealed; nor hid that shall not be known" (St. Matthew 10:26).

(2) There are several reasons why sin always becomes known, sooner or later, often in this world, but surely in the next, even if we escape exposure in this life. "Conscience makes cowards of us all." If we have guilty hearts, something in our action will betray us. Everyday life is full of slips of this kind, which give us away, and show to the world about us the very shame we most desire to hide. Those who sin with us, in one way or another, are more than likely to betray us. And there is a deep human need in every one of us to tell someone what we have done. Then, too, I need not remind you that some sins have physical consequences, which are part of the temporal punishment due for them.

(3) But it is not because of these inevitable and unavoidable consequences, in the physical or social realm, that we should fear sin, but because of the spiritual devastation which it works in the soul. Mortal sin, we say, kills the soul; not, of course as regards its immortality, but as regards its supernatural life. And if we lose that, we lose everything. Hell is nothing more nor less than the everlasting loss of God. Its other punishments are, so to speak, incidental; from which we can dimly see how terrible must be that pain of loss which is the chief torment of the damned. No physical or temporal punishment which sin may bring in its wake, can be nearly so terrible as the spiritual penalties which follow disobedience to the known law of God. As we fear death itself, so ought we to fear sin, which is so much more dreadful.

Peroration: In our madness and folly, deceived by the devil, blinded by temptation, we think when we sin that we are "living the life." Evil holds out all sorts of pleasant and advantageous lures, appears to us falsely and deceptively as something good and desirable. Yet sad experience should have taught us long ago that the devil is a liar, and that the results and consequences of sin, yes even sin itself, is far other than we, in the moment of temptation, had pictured in anticipation. As we look back afterwards we realize that we have been duped, fooled; that even the pleasures of sin were not what we had expected them to be, and that the inevitable results of sin are a price altogether too high to pay for what we have had.

Exactly the opposite is true of goodness. He who, by the grace and help of God, leads a good life, resists temptation, avoids sin and practices virtue, has no fear that his innermost secrets may become known to the world. He has nothing to hide, nothing for which to be ashamed, the peace of a good conscience is his in this world, and he has sure confidence and holy hope of salvation in the world to come.

Subject this matter to the judgment of your sober common sense. Do you not see that it does not pay to sin, and that it does pay to live a good life? Reason tells you that, without any revelation from God at all. Then God speaks, makes known His law, proclaims His rewards for virtue and His punishments for sin. Surely in the face of both Reason and Faith, we can no longer delude ourselves about this matter of sin and its consequences.

Eighth Sunday After Pentecost

(Romans 8:12) Brethren, we are debtors, not to the flesh, to live according to the flesh.

From birth to death, our bodies are insistent in their demands, we are always conscious of them, we must, in all things right, accede to them. Food, drink, rest, exercise, proper protection, due recreation, are demands of our physical nature which must be heeded, in which there is no harm, rather good, in heeding if moderation be observed in all things. God has created us not pure spirits, like the angels, nor mere physical animals, like the brutes, but a compound of body and soul, each side or part of our nature having its right use and its proper function in the life which we live in this world. If we speak of the soul as "our higher nature," and the body as "lower," it is no derogation of the wisdom of God, who made us as we are, and gave us, in the body rightly used, the best possible environment for the sanctification and salvation of the immortal soul which dwells therein.

(1) But, we must never forget that our bodies are the servants of our souls, that they have their right and proper place in the scheme of life, and that they must never for one moment be permitted to usurp the place of superiority over the soul, for which they were created to be but the tabernacle and minister. Because human nature is fallen, because human nature is weak, because the body, undisciplined, will always seek to usurp the foremost place, it is well for us frequently to remind ourselves of the purpose of life, the real reason why we have bodies, to

use, not abuse, to serve the soul, not to rule it or drag it down into eternal ruin.

(2) The physical sins, gluttony, sloth, and impurity (which is commonly regarded as especially "the sin of the fles ") all of them consist in the abuse of the bodily functions in some way contrary to the law of God. As food is necessary to the life of the body, but in excess is harmful, so the taking of food, which is a good thing in itself, may become sinful, either by inordinate pampering of the appetite, or because of a positive law regarding it. For example, there is nothing wrong, in itself, in a good beefsteak. But you may sin by eating too much steak, more than you need, or by eating it on a day when the ecclesiastical law forbids the use of meat.

So also with repose, the necessary rest which the body requires in order to repair the waste of tissue and energy from day to day. Sleep is a necessity of life, and a good thing in itself. But too much rest, or repose which interferes with duty, becomes sinful. The same truth holds good with regard to those functions of our physical nature which God has given us for His own good purposes in perpetuating the human race and providing subjects for the Sacraments of Holy Church. Those physical functions are good and holy in themselves; their use, under certain circumstance, is blessed and even commanded by Holy Church. Marriage is a Sacrament, the marriage relationship a good and holy thing. But we are forbidden under pain of mortal sin to exercise those functions outside of marriage.

(3) One rule of life, then, is the law of God, and not primarily the necessities of our bodily nature. Anything which hinders the soul, which bring sin upon it through disobedience to the law of God, is sinful and wrong. If the body demands certain things which are forbidden, it is to be sternly denied, disciplined, kept its right and proper place. We owe nothing more to the body than prudent and proper care. We do not owe it sinful indulgence of its inordinate appetite. We do not

owe it more than God permits it to claim for its proper well-being that it may further the eternal destinies of the soul. It is folly, and it is untrue, to say that we "have to" do this, or "have to have that" for the sake of our bodily comfort or health, when "this" or "that" is forbidden by the law of God. Our first duty is to the soul, our first concern must be for the soul, even if the body must be denied, kept in its place, punished, disciplined.

Peroration: It is the utmost importance that we have a sane and sanctified view of these vital matters. We naturally gravitate to physical ease and pleasure, it is easier for us to live what might be called "a natural life" than to keep ourselves always in the enjoyment of the supernatural life. But sinful indulgence is not only forbidden by the law of God, it is forbidden by the natural law as well, and observance of the Commandments is found, by experience, to be conducive to physical health and well-being no less than to the health and well-being of the soul.

Ninth Sunday After Pentecost

(1 Corinthians 10:12) Wherefore he that thinketh himself to stand, let him take heed lest he fall.

"Pride," we are told by the wise old philosopher who wrote the Book of Proverbs, "goeth before destruction: and the spirit is lifted up before a fall." And this text of Scripture has passed through misquotation into the popular saying. "Pride goes before a fall." There is nothing surprising in this, for pride was the sin of Satan and the rebel angels by which they lost Heaven and fell as deep as hell itself. Back of the disobedience of our first parents was pride that dared flout the command of God. It is the same with every sin that we commit: at bottom it is pride. And certainly, as we look back over our life, and recall, with shame, the many times we have made fools of ourselves, or have permitted the devil to make fools of us and to draw us into sin. We can very clearly see that just before the fatal act we were lifted up with pride, conceit, and self-sufficiency. One of the most humiliating things about repentance is the knowledge which it brings of how we might have avoided the sin. How we walked grandly on, our heads in the air, till the pit yawned at our feet: how sure we were that, though others had failed, we would not fail: how we trusted to strength of character to see us through instead of praying to God to assist our weakness. Then came the sin, and our pride was humbled in the dust.

(1) Human nature is so constituted that each individual man finds himself at the center of the universe, the whole world surrounding him. As children we become accustomed

to being served and waited upon, the center of a little family group which is, indeed, our world. But, little by little, we discover that there are others in the world besides ourselves, outside our little orbit, and that they may be, and are, much more important than we. Unless we learn this lesson of life, we remain children to the end. Other wills make themselves felt, and we must learn to obey. Normally the tyrant of the nursery becomes himself and a member of a family group, giving and taking like the rest. But as life goes on, most of us find ourselves once more in a commanding position, though there may be but one person for us to command. We discover, or fancy that we discover in ourselves some gift, physical strength or beauty; mental powers which distinguish us, more or less, from those about us, ability, skill or cleverness, of one sort or another. Immediately we take the credit to ourselves, "pride ourselves" on what we are, or what we can do, and begin to lord it over less fortunate persons. Then, suddenly, comes a catastrophe. Some-one more clever than we comes along and shows our ability to be but mediocre. We are humiliated and those over whom we have lorded it for a brief space breathe a sigh of relief.

(2) Before temptation comes upon us in its strength, we may fancy ourselves rather good people, look down upon others who show their weaknesses and faults, proclaim ourselves superior to this or that vice. "I should never stoop low," we say. Indeed, we express our scorn for the weaklings who have never felt. Then, in a moment, we fall; fall, it may be, into some sin far more terrible than that which we have reprobated in others. Our boasted character, in which we trusted, fails to stand the test. Some hidden and (by us) unsuspected weakness comes out to our undoing. Again we are humiliated, yet any of our friends could have told us the danger we were in, for they saw us as we really were, recognized the weakness that was hidden from us by our pride, knew that we were quite capable of doing the very things from which we had claimed

immunity into a mirror; you do not see yourself, as you really are, but all reversed, left for right. That is why one seldom satisfied with a portrait, which one's friends recognize to be a good likeness. But others see us as we are, and they are not surprised when we fall into this mistake, yield to that weakness, prove weak in a crisis. We are surprised, not they. What blinded us? Pride. So pride brought us to our fall.

(3) It is well for us to realize that we have, each one of us, within our nature the germs of every possible sin, that there is nothing in the whole catalogue of evil that we cannot do. Thank God, we are not tempted to every sin, but the very fact that we do fall into those which tempt us, should teach us a lesson in humility. Why should I think myself better than another, because he does this, and I have never even wished to do it. Perhaps I do far worse things. Perhaps, had I his temptations, I would fall far lower than he. What do I know of his struggle? Who am I to look down upon him? Am I so sure of myself? Do I think of myself to stand to firmly that I cannot fall. Beware, that is pride! I am on the brink; another moment and I shall be humbled in the dust.

Peroration: Self-sufficienc is a very insidious and a very dangerous form of pride, and it is the cause of most, if not all, of our falls from virtue into sin. We fancy we can resist any temptation, trust in our own strength and so neglect to make use of the grace of God, in the power of which alone we can conquer. "Without Me you can do nothing," said our Blessed Lord (St. John 15:15); no, not so much as think anything of ourselves, adds St. Paul (2 Corinthians 3:5), but our sufficiency is of God. Only by His grace and help can we resist temptation, only with His aid fight the battle against sin, only under His protection stand secure. But if we depend utterly upon God, if we cooperate with the graces He gives us, if we rely solely upon His help in time of need, then indeed we not only think, but know that we stand and need fear no fall, so long as we are united to Him. "I can do all things in Him who strengtheneth me" (Philippians 4:13).

Tenth Sunday After Pentecost

(1 Corinthians 12:11) But all these things one and the same Spirit worketh, dividing to every one according to His will.

We are accustomed to speaking of certain persons as "gifted" or "having talent" in one way or another, meaning that they show an aptitude for art, or music, or in some trade or profession, which peculiarly fits them for the work which they have undertaken. In ordinary life we recognize that this spe-cial talent or gift may have very little connection with the ordinary environment of an individual, or may be more or less directly traced to a similar aptitude on the part of the family, according to circumstances. Sometimes several members of the same household may become priests or religious, again a thoroughly worldly family may produce a priest and a thoroughly good family may be grieved that none of its members have a "vocation." But, when you come to think of it, everybody has a vocation to something, some work, some career, sacred or secular, which he seems peculiarly fitted to follow. And it is clearly indicated in Holy Scripture that God has some special and particular work for each one of us to do in this world, and that by doing that work we shall more easily and surely save our souls.

(1) We must not expect a special revelation from God regarding our vocation, or wait for some voice to speak within us, directing us infallibly to the task which is to be our life-work. An absorbing interest in some trade or profession may be the only indication that that is our proper "gift." Evident ability in a certain line, the advice of competent people who know our capabilities. Physical or

mental strength, and so on:—these are the guide-posts which lead us to the conclusion that our vocation lies in this field or that, as the case may be. If it is a matter of a vocation, in the strict sense, to the priesthood or the religious life, there are easily recognized signs, which a prudent confessor will explain to you if you are seriously interested in the matter. With regard to the secular vocations, each must judge more or less for himself, after seeking advice from those who know him, and who also know the work upon which he is thinking of entering.

(2) If a person has certain talents or gifts, it is incumbent upon him to make good use of them. They may be for the good of his soul, or just the opposite. For example, musical ability, which may be offered to God in the service of the Church, exercised for the innocent pleasure of one's friends, or employed in such bad ways that it becomes an occasion of sin to the possessor and others. The e is no aptitude or ability which cannot be used to the honor and glory of God, by virtue of a right intention, for we are bidden to offer to God all the we are, all that we do. (see 1 Corinthians 10:31). For all that we are, all that we have, of skill or cleverness, or intellectual power, manual dexterity, artistic taste, is a gift from God, and to be used, directly or indirectly in His service, and for the good of souls, our own and others.

(3) Just as we learn by experience that there are certain things we can do well, with but little practice, or better than others do them, so we find out after a while that there are other things that we cannot do, try we ever so hard. We sometimes see the sad sight of a man or woman who has, as the saying goes "missed his calling," who is trying to do some work for which he is obviously unfitted both by nature and training, and consequently making a failure of it. Perhaps he has gone in for that particular work from wrong motives, perhaps he has not improved his opportunities to learn his trade or profession thoroughly,

having been lazy and careless; perhaps, through no fault of his own, he has been forced into his present position by circumstances. "Happy is the man who has found his work," says poor Richard. Equally true, unhappy is the man who is doing work for which he is fitted neither by nature nor by grace.

Peroration: You see, then, how important it is, both for usefulness and happiness in this world, and even for salvation, to find the work that God wants you to do, and then to do it with all your might. Whatever your vocation in this world may be, whatever the work which you have elected to perform, you owe it to yourself, nay, you owe it to God, to do it just as well as lies in you, offering the doing of it to God, praying for His help and guidance, giving Him the glory for whatever success may crown your efforts. You young people should ponder well the life-work which lies before you, not entering upon this trade or that profession just because it is easy and agreeable, not turning away from work which you could do well just because it is difficult or entails some time of preparation. And every one of you, boy or girl, should ask yourself seriously whether or not it may be God's will for you to embrace a higher state of life. Don't be afraid to ask advice from those who know you, and also know something of the sort of work you think you want to do. Don't be discouraged if you make mistakes and false starts, and have to begin all over again. But pray to the Holy Ghost to guide you into the right use of the gifts and talents which He Himself has bestowed upon you.

Eleventh Sunday After Pentecost

(1 Corinthians 15:10) But by the grace of God I am who I am, and His grace in me hath not been void.

Nothing is more certain than that man has a nature prone to evil as the result of the Fall of our First Parents, and that he can, of himself, do but little towards overcoming the downward drag of that disability which persists even when, by Baptism, he is raised to the supernatural state. Exterior temptations are not lacking, the world and the devil are constantly seeking to compass the ruin of souls. Left to himself, man would inevitably and repeatedly fall into actual sin. But God, in His mercy, does not leave His children helpless in the lifelong battle for virtue. Again and again He offers His grace, His supernatural assis-tance, at every crisis of life, in every pressure of temptation, and by this divine help it is possible for those who cooperate with it to remain in the state of grace, to battle successfully with the enemies of the soul, and live a godly, just, and sober life.

(1) "Without me you can do nothing" (St. John 15:5), says our Blessed Lord, and sad experience proves the truth of the words. The strongest and most upright character, without the help of God is doomed to fall victim to sin, and even the "splendid virtues" of the pagan and the godless must ever lack that element of supernatural motive which makes them meritorious. This being true, the complementary truth must also be stressed, that with the help of God all things are possible, the very heights of sanctity in reach of all. "With men this is impossible: but with God all things are possible" (St Matthew 19:26).

(2) The grace and help of God are freely offe ed and freely given to all who need and seek them. The e is not an exigency of life for which God will not give the appropriate and necessary grace. The wonderful system of the Sacraments, instituted by Christ and administered by the Catholic Church, is the chief evidence of this, for from the cradle to the brink of the grave there is not a crisis of life for which some Sacrament is not offe ed to give the needed assistance to the weakness of our mortal nature. In infancy we are raised to the supernatural order, in childhood strengthened by the gift of the Holy Ghost in Confirmation. For our lapses from virtue, which deprive us of sanctifying grace, there is Penance, which not only restores us to the friendship of God, but also revives all the graces previously received. Are we confronted by an important change in our state of life, God stands there to bless it and give the graces needed for the new duties we undertake, whether it be in the married state, or in the holy priesthood. Are we menaced by death, Extreme Unction makes it possible for us to meet this last and most important crisis with equanimity. And every day of our life the Blessed Sacrament is our food and strength, the upbuilding of the eternal structure of grace, the safeguard against temptations, the earnestness of everlasting happiness.

(3) With all this being done for us by Almighty God, why is it that we so frequently fall away from the virtue which He rightly expects of us, which he makes possible for us, and for which, if we are in earnest at all, we should be constantly striving? The answer is simple: we do not make full use of the graces bestowed upon us, or we are negligent in receiving them when we need them most. For we can refuse the help of God, through pride, which foolishly trusts in self to do the work that only God can do; through carelessness or sloth or downright malice. It is a terrible thought that all this great outpouring of grace can be "in vain" for us, unless we co-operate with it, appropriate it to ourselves, and make good use of it once it has

been bestowed.

Peroration: St. Paul, like every other saint, ascribes his goodness to the help of God. We, though far from being saints, must do the same. But we can only blames ourselves if we are not good. Which is more to be wondered at,—that, with so many means of grace at hand, we are still so bad; or, in view of the temptations of life, we are by God's help as decent as we are? Without God's constant help we would be the most terrible sinners in the world. Even with it, we are not what we ought to be, what we could be, did we but make better use of the divine assistance offe ed and given us. How soon we forfeit grace received, simply because we do not exercise it, do not "stir up the grace of God which is in" us (2 St. Timothy, 1:6). Pray that God, who gives His grace so abundantly, may give also the grace to make full use of it, so that St. Paul's humble boast may be ours as well.

Twelfth Sunday After Pentecost

(2 Corinthians 3:5) Not that we are sufficient to think anything of ourselves, as of ourselves: but our sufficiency is of God.

What helpless creatures we are! Entering this world in infantile weakness, we must be carried about, nursed, cared for in every way for a long time before we are able to do the most simple things for ourselves. All through childhood we depend on others for the necessities of life; even in youth we must look to others for instruction, help, support. Adult life brings a certain measure of responsibility and self-reliance, but even the best of us must depend upon the help of others in more ways than we realize until we give the matter careful thought. Consider how many people it takes to make possible your daily life. What would your business be without the cooperation of others, your home without the other members of your family? So we might go on showing how, all through life, we are dependent, to a greater or less degree, upon those round about us, and even upon the work of many whom we never see and rarely think about. When illness or old age bring us into danger of death, once more we become utterly dependent upon the ministrations of others, and so we pass out of life, helpless, as we entered it.

(1) If this is true of our bodily life, it is even more so of our intellectual life. We like to believe that we "think ourselves," but a moment's study will show us how greatly we depend on others even for our thoughts. The experience of each one is limited, the knowledge of each is small compared with the intellectual wealth of the world. No one can know everything

about any one subject, or even something about every subject. So we share our knowledge, and much that we say we know, we actually accept on the authority of others without having any first-hand knowledge of it at all. Children gain their working-knowledge of the world beyond their own narrow horizon from teachers and books. The son usually accepts his father's religion and politics as his own without much personal investigation. We are all accustomed to respect the dicta of scientific and professional men in their own recognized fields, and in certain exigencies of life we consult them, as the physician when we are ill, the lawyer when we are involved in legal matters, the priest when we need religious guidance.

(2) It is here, perhaps, that most of us are quite willing to admit our ignorance. Home remedies may be all very well for little indispositions, but let anything be seriously the matter with us, and we call in the doctor. We have some light understanding of the process of law, but what non-professional man would think of going into court to try a suit, or to plead his own case. We employ experts for these things and we feel no shame in admitting our ignorance. In religious and moral matters we realize that we must have guidance. Even those who profess to find their religion in "the bible and the Bible only," listen with respect to the ministers they employ to expound the Sacred Text, while we who have the true Church for our teacher are quite willing to sit humbly at her feet and learn from her necessary lessons which, as children of God, we must know in order to live good lives and save our souls.

(3) If, then, we are so dependent upon our fellow-creatures, how much more are we dependent upon God! Even life itself would not be ours were it not for His gift, and when He wills it, we shall die. The most insignificant circumstances of our life are of His ordering and it is only as He sustains His creation that we are able to go on with the manifold interests and activities which so engross us that, more often than not, we fail to

realize how absolutely and utterly dependent we are upon the Providence of God. When we think of the supernatural life of the soul, we see that all this is a thousandfold true. For were it not for the continual outpouring of God's grace upon our souls, surely we know that we could not remain for a moment in a condition pleasing to Him and safe for ourselves. Not only does God give us the actual graces we need at every moment of our life, but in the Sacraments He bestows upon us whatever measure of sanctifying grace we may need. There is not a crisis, not a great event of our life, but what the appropriate and necessary Sacrament is provided to bless and sanctify it. Baptism brings sanctifying grace to the soul at the very outset of its earthly life. When childhood gives place to youth, with its dan-gers and temptations, Confirmation is our strength. Does mortal sin deprive us of grace? Penance restores it to us once more. Frequently, even daily, our Blessed Lord comes to us in the Blessed Sacrament to flood us with the grace of which He is the Author. Would we change our state of life, either by marriage or by entering the priesthood, Matrimony and Holy Orders are special Sacraments to give the special graces required for special needs. And at the end, when all help and assistance save that of God is vain, Extreme Unction assures us that our souls are in His favor and ready to meet Him as our Judge and Saviour.

Peroration: Were it not for these blessed facts, how could we dare to face life, with its dangers to soul and body, its constant temptations, its overwhelming sorrows and trials, its pressing duties? Well might the Apostle cry out, confronted with the fear of life, and the tremendous task of securing the soul's salvation in spite of such terrible odds, "for these things who is sufficient? (2 Corinthians 12:9), and again, "I can do all things in Him who strengtheneth me" (Philippians 4:13). With such assurances of God's loving care and protection, need we fear? Shall we not rather cast all our care upon Him and trust Him for all we need.

Thirteenth Sunday After Pentecost

(Galatians 3:22) But the scripture hath concluded all under sin, that the promise by the faith of Jesus Christ might be given to them that believe.

Sin is one of the commonest experiences of life, something that mars and spoils and upsets us all. We look at some beautiful little child, so pure and good, and we realize that in a few short years sin will have left its mark on that unfolding character. We contemplate the saint, whose life of goodness has been a help and inspiration to so many, and yet we know that in the past, sin has had some part, however slight, in the career of that soul. For, as Holy Scripture tells us so plainly, "all have sinned, and do need the glory of God" (Romans 3:23). Of Mary alone, among all humanity, can it be said with absolute certainty, that never sin passed upon her, original or actual, mortal or venial.

(1) This universal fact of sin, which we see all about us and in everyone we know, to a greater or less degree, is terrible enough, but it would be infinitely more awful did we not recall the further and consoling fact that Christ died for sinners. His satisfaction for sin upon the Cross was so tremendous, so divine, that it could avail for all, no matter how wicked, if only they would appropriate it, coöperate with it, make it their own. For God has held nothing back either in promising or fulfi‐ ment. If men go on sinning, it is because they do not make use of the graces God offers them to amend; if souls are lost at the last, it is because they have not availed themselves of the salvation offe ed them by Christ Himself.

(2) Who is there that would dare claim to be sinless? Who would presume to think that God's grace and help were unnecessary to him, that he could win Heaven by his own unaided effo ts, or overcome temptation solely by the strength of his character? And yet how many there are who act as if they both claimed sinlessness and disdained the assistance of God? How quick we are to deny our faults and weaknesses, faults and weaknesses which everyone knows to be ours. How careless we are of receiving the means of grace, how prone to trust to ourselves rather than to God in an emergency. Worst of all, how ready we are to excuse ourselves by saying, "I couldn't help it," when we are overcome by temptation and fall into sin. What a childish excuse! And it is not true, for as we look back we can see how we might have avoided the occasion of sin, might have fortified ourselves against it, might, indeed, not have committed the sin at all.

(3) For one of the promises of God to us, His children, is that no irresistible temptation shall ever be permitted to overwhelm us. Always, when temptation comes, God will make "issue," that is to say, a way of escape, that by His grace and help we may overcome it and turn it into a victory (see 1 Corinthians 10:13). We do not have sin. Our wills are free, even in the greatest stress of temptation, and only when we consent to temptation, does it become sin. Remember the definition of mortal sin which you learned in your Catechism, and you will see that you cannot sin inadvertently, or without the full consent of your will. No matter how sudden or strong the temptation, there is always the chance to invoke the help of God, to fall back on His grace, to claim His promise of help and assistance.

Peroration: God does not help us in some automatic or magical manner; nor will He save us against our will and without our cooperation. We must "with fear and trembling work out (our) salvation" (Philippians 2:12). We know how God desires to help us; we know that He places at our disposal tremendous forces of divine grace; but if through carelessness, indifference, or downright malice, we refuse to make use of God's help, we shall have no one but ourselves to blame if we wake up some fine morning and find ourselves in hell! It is no use to say, "I have the Faith, I'll not be lost." Faith without works is dead, and the Faith will certainly not save you unless you practice it. Shall we not, then, resolve to be practical Catholics, making full use of the Sacraments and of prayer, which are the chief means of bringing God's grace to our souls, thus fighting the daily battle against temptation, not in our own strength, but with God's own weapons, and so assuring ourselves of victory?

Fourteenth Sunday After Pentecost

(Galatians 5:24) They that are Christ's have crucified their flesh with the vices and concupiscences.

So long as life shall last, we are bound, both by religion and reason, to keep up a continual struggle against whatever is evil and vicious in our fallen human nature. In saying this we do not admit that any natural appetite or function is evil in itself. Having been created, and its proper use ordained, by Almighty God, both reason and religion teach us that the body is good and holy. It is the wrong use of bodily appetites, the unreasonable indulgence and abuse of them, which is sinful. Theology teaches us that "concupiscence," that is the desire to exercise any bodily function, is not in itself sinful. Nevertheless, it must be controlled, kept in its place, restricted to its proper and lawful use, or it will become the occasion of sin.

(1) Because our human nature is fallen, because we, so to speak, inherit from our First Parents a tendency to excess in the use of physical pleasures; because, therefore, it is easier for us to fall into sin than it is for us to maintain virtue; and also (and this is most important) because both the natural and the divine law forbid the use of certain things, under certain circumstances, we are bound to restrain ourselves, to fight against the propensity to excess, to keep ourselves within the limits allowed to us by the Commandments of God. This is not easy; it is, indeed, what St. Paul calls it, a veritable crucifixion of the flesh. But even unaided reason, without any revelation from God, teaches us that such a battle, such a conquest of self, is the

only way to true happiness even in this world.

(2) For we see all around us the evidence of the deplorable consequences of unbridled appetite, unrestricted yielding to the demands of the body. The fatal results of intemperance, lust, anger, and the life, are only too well known to us. We have seen lives ruined by them, we have seen homes destroyed, the bright promise of youth brought to nothing, disease and death brought on by nothing else than excess or the unlawful use of some bodily function which ought to have been kept under control and disciplined into its proper place, but which has, instead, been weakly yielded to, until it dominated the life and dragged the man down below the level of the brutes. The "crime waves" which periodically sweep across the country; the drink evil; the social evil; what are these but the results of lack of self-discipline and self-control? Common sense ought to tell us how fatal self-indulgence, in any of these things, must inevitably prove to be.

(3) But the Christian, the Catholic, has a far higher motive for virtue than the mere worldling, a more cogent reason for austerity than the person who restrains his appetite simply because he realizes that over-indulgence in drink, or the pleasure of the table, or reckless extravagance in the exercise of any other bodily function, is going to injure his health or bring him to disgrace. We have the positive and revealed law of God for our guide; but more than this, we are taught that in Baptism we are made members of the body of Christ, identified with Him in a real though mystical manner, so that our sins are an injury to God, an insult to our Creator, which must inevitably bring a punishment far more terrible than even those dreadful results which outraged nature must suffer in this world

Peroration: So, as Christians, as Catholics, we are called upon to restrain and keep within their proper and legitimate bounds, each and all of the bodily appetites which clamor for satisfaction, and which are the cause of so many of our temptations and trials. The harder this is for us to do, the more merit there will be in our doing of it, and, be it said, the greater will be the graces given us by God to enable us to do it. For God does not ask us to do what is impossible, He does not set before us a commandment that we cannot keep, but in His love and His kindness He gives us grace to fortify our weakness, which, if only we will use it, will surely give us the victory. The e is only one thing that is stronger than the desires of human nature, and that is grace. Grace is ever at our disposal, but it is necessary for us to do our part, to exert our wills, to take such precautions against occasions of sin as we know will help us to avoid temptation. And we know that if we earnestly strive, by God's help, to fight this lifelong battle we shall at last wear the crown that only follows the cross.

Fifteenth Sunday After Pentecost

(Galatians 6:10) Whilst we have time, let us work good to all men, but specially to those who are of the household of the faith.

Divine Law is the law of love. When our Blessed Lord was asked which Commandment is the greatest, He summarized them all into the twofold precept of love of God, and of the neighbor. The Old Dispensation was one of fear, the New Dispensation is one of love. In both the law is the same, and it can never change because it is the divine law and its principles are therefore immutably true and binding forever under all circumstances. But the motive for obedience, under the New Law of Christ, is no longer the ancient fear of punishment, but the gentle pressure of love, the desire to serve and please God because He is so infinitely good and so deserving of all our love, because sin is displeasing to Him, because by obedience we can best manifest our real and deep love for Him.

(1) But love is not a mere emotion of the heart, it is also an act of the will. If this were not so, it would be unreasonable for our Lord to command us to love God and our neighbor. "Thou shalt love" (St. Matthew 22:37) implies that it is within our power to elicit an act of love even when our emotions are not concerned. The force of this is still more apparent when we remember that we are commanded to love even our enemies (St. Matthew 5:44). The fraternal charity, therefore, which we are bound in conscience to extend even to those who are furthest from returning it, is something greater than feeling, emotion, affection in the ordinary sense of the word. And it is, moreover,

something of which we are perfectly capable, by the assistance of divine grace, even when we do not, and cannot, produce those feelings which are usually associated with what we call "love" in its usual sense.

(2) Charity, or love (for the words mean the same thing), is not content to remain passive. It is not enough, even with regard to our enemies, that we should refrain from returning their evil with evil, but we must be ever ready to help and assist them, to be a positive benefit to them and this in spite of what they have done against us. (see 1 St. Peter 3:9 also I Thessalonians 5:15) This is, perhaps, one of the most difficul of the teachings of our Blessed Lord to follow, yet we have both His positive command and the force of His example to show us how very necessary it is. He prayed for His enemies, as His saints did after Him, and the least work of charity that we can do towards those who have injured us is to give them a place in our prayers. But we ought, also, to go out of our way to be kind to those who have been unkind to us. So far from permitting thoughts and acts of revenge, we must seek opportunity to help those who have injured us, for by so doing we shall indeed heap coals upon their heads and, who knows?, make friends of them.

(3) If this is our duty towards those who have injured us; if we are to preserve Christian charity even towards those who are bound to us by no ties save those of duty; how much more are we bound to good works towards those who share with us the priceless blessings of "the household of Faith." The very fact that they are Catholics gives them a sort of spiritual relationship to us, a sort of claim upon us. All that has been said of our duty towards others is true a thousandfold more of our brethren in the Faith. Yet all too often we find ourselves indulging in bitter feelings towards them, even seeking to injure them. For shame! Are we not brethren, members of one family, bound together by ties of Religion even stronger than ties of blood can ever be? Daily we have opportunity to put into practice

this great virtue of charity towards those who share with us the priceless heritage of the Catholic Religion. Our family, our neighbors, the parish, the diocese, these have claims upon us which are founded on the divine law of charity, and we ignore them at our peril.

Peroration: But if charity begins at home, it is no true charity if it stops there. When we consider our Catholic neighbors, the neighborhood broadens to take in the whole world! It is on this score that the Church appeals to us all, as never before, for interest and assistance in her activities throughout the world. It is being borne in upon us, more and more strongly, that we have a duty to those of the Faith who are, perhaps, farthest from us, as the world counts distance, and least close, as the world counts resemblance. You can easily see the bearing of all this on the matter of appeals for help to the missions, in distant parts of our own land and in the foreign field. Never turn a deaf ear to such appeals, when they come to you vouched for by proper authority. Let your charity be universal as your Faith. If the demands seem many, remember that had not some noble missionary been imbued with just the sort of charity we have been imbued with, just the sort of charity we have been considering, our forefathers might never have received the light of Faith and we might, today, be without its blessings. "Freely have you received, freely give" (St. Matthew 10:8).

Sixteenth Sunday After Pentecost

(Ephesians 3:19) To know also the charity of Christ, which surpasseth all knowledge...

Remember that the word "charity" in Holy Scripture, is always synonymous with "love" in its fullest and best sense. Remember, also, that love is never to be confused with its counterfeit, passion, but is always pure, noble, unselfish. If only we can clarify our conception of love, we shall certainly be better and happier, for we are so apt to mistake the imitation for the real thing, and suffer in consequence

The love of Christ for our souls is the greatest thing in the world. It is what called Him from His eternal throne in Heaven, to come into this world to live, suffer and die for us. The whole story of the Incarnation is summed up in one phrase, "Sic dilexit Deus mundum, God so loved the world" (St. John 3:16).

(1) We have every reason for knowing the love of Christ for us, for we have heard the divine story of it since we were able to understand human speech, we have had experience of it from the moment of our Baptism till now, and every time we look at the Crucifix, or attend Holy Mass, or bless ourselves, or, indeed, perform any religious act, we are reminded of the love of the Sacred Heart for us poor sinners. In a sense, of course, we can never fully understand Christ's love for us, for our hearts and minds are finite and His love is infinite But in the sense of knowing it because we experience it, our whole life is a school to teach us how great, how wonderful,

how patient, how enduring is the love which our dear Lord showers upon us.

(2) For what is our whole life, with the sole exception of the sin which mars and spoils it, but a constant proof of Christ's love for us? Nay, even our sins bring that love out all the stronger, for it is because of His great love that we find pardon for sin and the strength to amend our lives by His grace. Even our suffering is a proof of His love, "for whom the Lord loveth, He chastiseth; and He scourgeth every son whom He receiveth" (Hebrews 12:6). It is that His love may spare us the eternal punishment which we, by our sins, have deserved, that He graciously permits us to suffer meritoriously in this life. Temptations? Yes, they also may be proofs of His love, for it is when we turn to Him in the stress of temptation that He pours our His grace to enable us to resist and so turn temptation into victory and gain merit for our souls. But what of the sorrows of life? Surely if Christ loves us, He would wish all our life to be gay and happy and uncrossed by shadows. Not so! He was a Man of Sorrows (Isaias 53:3), and experience shows us how it is most often in our sorrows that we are drawn closest to His broken Heart. Indeed, it sometimes happens that if our dear Lord can take His place in our human hearts in no other way, He will break them, and so find entrance

(3) Just as we cannot know the fullness and joy of human love until we find an answer to our affection in the heart of another, or until we respond to the love which is offe ed to us, so we shall never fully experience the love of the Sacred Heart for us until we return it by the giving of our own complete devotion. Jesus cries to us, out of the depths of His undying love, "My son, give Me thy heart" (Proverbs 23:26). And we cannot know how Jesus loves us, unless and until we heed that cry and give Him all our love, poor and human as it is, in return for His eternal and divine love. This is (as we have seen—Sermon for the Fifteenth Sunday after Pentecost) not a mere matter of

emotion. Along with love comes duty, and the proof of love is action. "If you love Me, keep My Commandments" (St. John 14:15). Actions speak louder than words, and God, no less than those we love on earth, must have something more than just the words, "I love you."

Peroration: If we do not come, more and more, all through our life, "to know the charity of Christ," it is because we willfully and sinfully turn away from it and refuse it. "Unrequited love" in the human sense, has passed into a proverb, and most of us know how bitter it is to give our affection where it is not appreciated and returned. How dreadful the thought of those to whom Jesus Christ has offe ed His love, and who have refused it. Instead of being drawn to Him by all He has done for them, they hate Him for it. Or worse, they are indifferent to it, preferring the fleeting happiness of earth to the eternal joys of Heaven, throwing themselves into the enjoyment of that "counterfeit love" which leads to sin and hell, rather than returning to the calm, pure, uplifting love to which the Sacred Heart calls them, and which, in their better moments, they must know is the only true and real lasting love. May it not be said of us that we have turned a deaf ear to the pleading of the Sacred Heart, refused His love, wounded Him by our carelessness, our coldness, our disobedience, our sin. Rather shall we not go on, by the path of love, to know Him better and serve Him more faithfully in this world so that when at last we come into His presence we may say, "I know whom I have believed" (2 St. Timothy 1:12) ?

Seventeenth Sunday After Pentecost

(Ephesians 4:5) One Lord, one faith, one baptism.

Unity, as we remember from our Catechism, is one of the notes or marks by which the true church, founded by Jesus Christ, may be distinguished from the welter of man-made sects which have arisen since the sixteenth century to claim the title of "Churches." The Catholic Church is the only body of organized Christians which can show, besides the marks of Holiness, Universality and Apostolicity, the distinction of teaching One faith, everywhere and always, and of being ruled by one divinely appointed Head. Division is the mark by which we recognize Protestantism, its hundreds of sects, approximately one for every year of its existence, dividing it to such an extent that it would be extremely difficult to answer the question. "What is Protestantism?" while any child can define the Catholic Church in a single sentence.

(1) God is not the author of confusion; division and discord among those who profess to be His worshippers are not any part of His plan for saving the world. So transcendently important is the salvation of the souls of men, that He could not leave them without a sure and certain guide as to how they may assure themselves of that salvation and share in its benefits in this world as well as the next. As God is one, so must His Church, which is the teacher of His truth, be one. NO one doubts that in Old Testament times there was but one true religion, one true Church. To the Jews God gave His ancient revelation, entrusted His worship, promised redemption. This does not mean that there were

not elements of truth in even the most debased pagan religions. St. Paul, preaching to the pagans of Lycaonia, tells them that, even in the old pagan days and among heathen peoples, God "left not Himself without testimony" (Acts 16:16). All had some partial truth, as it were a glimpse of God, albeit clouded and obscured by the ancient superstition of the Gentiles. But only the Jewish Church was the true church of God, only it had the complete revelation of God insofar as it had then been given.

(2) Nor can any reasonable man, reading the New Testament and studying history, find the least evidence that our Blessed Lord established more than one Church. Until the sixteenth century no one dreamed that there could be any other Church than the Catholic, or that anyone less than God could found a church. True, there were heresies and schisms, but none of them made any claim to being the Church founded by Christ. Each had, it may be, some fragment of truth, overlaid with the errors of men. None of them held the truth in its entirety, and the test of orthodoxy was ever unity, the holding of the one faith, and submission to the one center of authority, the Holy See. The rebellion of proud men, renegade priests some of them, alas, profligate monarchs, political self-seekers all, sought to explain away the plain words of Scripture and to deny the evident facts of history, setting up a new standard of religious organization, in which there could be no unity either of teaching, of leadership, or of government. Theend, after fewer than four hundred years, is the confusion of belief and practice which we see in the non-Catholic world. One denomination denies as foolish the very teaching another proclaims as essen-tial, until, looked upon as a whole, the negations of the various sects of Protestantism cancel out the whole creed.

(3) Unity of belief, coherence of teaching, cooperation in administration are obviously impossible under such circumstances. Aroused by the fearful waste of money and effo t which their unhappy divisions cannot avoid, our separated brethren

are today vainly searching for a basin of union. In spite of the fact that the old denominational diffeences have almost disappeared, due to the indiffeence of their people which is the inevitable result of such a strife of doctrine, it seems impossible for them to find any common ground upon which to unite, unless, perchance, it be the one thing which they hold in common, hatred of the Catholic Church. Some hold that Christ is Lord, yet explain away His Divinity, while others flatly deny it. Some administer Baptism as a sign of conversion, some few as a true Sacrament regenerating the soul; many fail to administer it at all, others, while telling us that it is unnecessary, insist that if it is received at all it may only be given in a particular form, which others do not practice. While as for faith: not only does one denomination differ from another to such an extent that their doctrines are mutually exclusive, but the slogan of private interpretation of the Bible practically brings into the being as many diffeent faiths as there are individual Protestants.

Peroration: In the midst of this "strife of tongues," this confusion of differing doctrines, this whirligig of varied organization, this constant flux and change of standards, the Catholic Church has stood like a rock, unmoved, calm, firm, enduring. For twenty centuries she has borne consistent witness to the one Faith, once for all delivered to the saints (St. Jude 3), teaching today exactly the same doctrine she proclaimed by the mouth of the Apostles who received it from her Divine Founder Himself, carrying on the same worship always and everywhere, under one government, looking to one supreme authority, which binds all together into one organism, which is nothing less than the Mystical Body of Christ (Ephesians 1:22-23). Even if the Church were mistaken, as her enemies claim, the world could not but admire such consistency, and as Mr. Chesterton has said, a Church which never went right, would be quite as much a miracle as a Church which never went wrong! What a blessing, what a privilege, to be members of that one true Church, worshippers of the one Christ, believers in the one Faith, recipients of the one Baptism by which we are made God's own children, regenerated, saved. It is a treasure never to be surrendered, proudly to be claimed, but never hoarded. Who, realizing its eternal worth would not seek to share it, chiefly by prayer, with those who do not have it?

Eighteenth Sunday After Pentecost

(1 Corinthians 1:4) Brethren, I give thanks to my God for you, for the grace of God is given you in Christ Jesus...

What is God's greatest gift to man? Certainly not his bodily capabilities, for man shares these with brutes. Nor can it be, even the wonderful faculties of his mind, for great though they are, by themselves, they could never bring him to eternal happiness in this life. Sanctifying grace—this is God's greatest gift to man, the gift he must treasure, increase, and render back to God at last in exchange for eternal glory.

(1) As the soul is, obviously, of more importance than the body, so the life of the soul is of supreme importance. Man having been raised to the supernatural state, given sanctifying grace and thus made acceptable to God, has the paramount duty of preserving that grace. It is ours, by virtue of our Baptism. Yet how soon we forfeit it by sin. For what do we exchange the friendship of God and the safety of our souls? A moment's pleasure; the brief admiration of our fellows; place and power which cannot last; money which we cannot take with us when this short life is over. What shall be said for our judgement of values, when we exchange our priceless heritage as children of God for such transitory and vanishing baubles as these! If we lose sanctifying grace, we lose God, we lose all. If we preserve sanctifying grace, what else matters, for, having god, we have all things.

(2) We are taught in our Catechism that the Sacraments of the Living increase sanctifying grace. Baptism bestows it,

Penance restores it when it is lost by sin. All other Sacraments increase it according to the need of the recipient in view of circumstances of his life. True, the grace of Baptism would save us if we preserved it through life and were unable to receive any sacrament. But, human nature being what it is, life so full of temptations, special graces, the goodness of God offers to us means for the necessary increase of sanctifying grace just when we need it most. The child, verging upon adolescence, receives Confirmation. The young couple, about to enter the married state, have a special Sacrament to give them the special assistance of grace; the young man about to bind himself to the onerous duties of the priesthood, receives in Holy Orders not only authority, but the grace necessary to exercise it; the old, the sick, the dying, face to face with the last grim journey, find in Extreme Unction such an increase of grace as shall carry them safely through the terror of darkness. And to us all, again and again, all our life long, our Blessed Lord comes in His most Blessed Sacrament, His hands filled with graces and blessings to comfort and support us till the end. What a wonderful story, the story of the grace of God which is given us!

(3) Great gifts imply equally great responsibilities, for "unto whomsoever much is given, of him much shall be required" (St. Luke 12:48). Having bestowed such an abundance of grace upon us, God has the right to expect great things from us in return. And we shall be held accountable for our use (or misuse) of grace. If we have lost it by sin, frustrated it by indifference and failure to correspond with it, failed to receive the Sacraments which bring it to us, or which augment it, for this we shall be judged. If, at the last, we go into God's presence without this gift of sanctifying grace in our souls, we shall be banished forever from that presence, and that will be hell. It is this that makes the Church so solicitous about what we call "the Last Sacraments," that none of her children may pass out of this life without sanctifying grace, and so be lost eternally.

But how shall we be sure that those last ministrations will be available to us? In the midst of the uncertainties, the dangers, the constant risks of life, we dare not take chances with death, which may overtake us at any moment. The e is only one safe and sure way, and that is never to forfeit sanctifying grace, never to remain, if we are so unhappy as to lose it by sin, out of the state of grace for one moment; to receive Sacraments frequently so that sanctifying grace may be protected against its loss. We cannot merit a good death, but we can live a good life and so be sure, humanly speaking, of dying with the grace of God unimpaired in our souls.

Peroration: Is it not worth while, then, to attend seriously to this great business of the salvation of our souls? What can be of greater importance than this? It is not an easy task, for we are surrounded by enemies who seek to rob us of sanctifying grace and to keep us from having it through life and in death. The world, the flesh, and the devil will cheat us out of salvation if they can, and the only thing which will prevent them from accomplishing their evil purpose is the constant presence of grace in our souls. We know that it is possible for a man to go through the whole of his life without ever once surrendering this divine gift. Nothing short of this should be our serious purpose. It is enable us to do this, to help us to save our souls, that Christ died, that the Church exists, so far as we are concerned. Shall we make all this go for nothing by our carelessness, indiffe ence, and actual sin?

Nineteenth Sunday After Pentecost

(Ephesians 4:25) Wherefore putting away lying, speak ye the truth every man to his neighbor: for we are members one of another.

One of the calumnious charges frequently brought against the Catholic Church by her enemies, is that she teaches her people that it is not a sin to lie, and so encourages dishonesty and hypocrisy. Of course, anyone who had ever taken the trouble to read a Catholic prayer book with its points for the examination of conscience before Confession; or who had investigated Catholic teaching at first hand by so simple a method as the perusal of the "penny catechism," would know that the Church has always been a staunch upholder of the sacredness of the Eighth Commandment of God, which forbids us to bear false witness, and thus makes lying a sin, which may be mortal. There are distinctions and classifications in all matters, there are different kinds of sin, there are circumstances which alter cases, and even the civil law recognizes these principles, and does not force a man to bear witness against himself. But we need not go into these details; it suffice that we reiterate the moral law of God, and of the Catholic Church, which forbids us to lie, and commands us to speak the truth.

(1) Any intelligent man who has read carefully the eighth section of the appendix to Cardinal Newman's great book, the Apologia, where he refutes in the most masterly manner this old calumny against the Catholic Church, and even shows that Protestant theologians have supported the very teaching for which the Church is unjustly reprobated, will be surprised that

this old attack against the Catholic Church still persists, and is even today put forward by those who hate what they suppose to be Catholicism. Unfortunately there is some basis for this misapprehension in the minds of non-Catholics, for, to our shame be it said, Catholics are often careless of the truth, and frequently fall into the sin of lying. But this does not mean that their Religion teaches them to lie; it only means that they are not good Catholics, and that they are not obeying the teachings of the Catholic Church. Non-Catholics are also guilty of this and other sins, but we would not dream of making the claim that the Protestant Religion teaches them to do such things.

(2) But, because our Religion is to so large an extent judged by our conduct, it behooves us to be exceedingly careful in this matter of speaking the truth. It is a fearful thing to bring discredit upon our Holy Mother the Church, and this we do when we forget or ignore her teaching, and do or say things which bring her into disgrace. You know the old saying, "Honesty is the best policy," and if you have had any experience of life at all, you know that there is hardly anything that so injures a man's reputation as carelessness regarding the truth. No higher praise can be given by the world than to say of a man, "His word is as good as his bond." The honest and upright man has the respect of all, and though he may occasionally have to suffer for his truthfulness, in the long run it will be found that veracity pays.

(3) These, however, are not the highest motives for truthfulness. Even the honor of Holy Church is not so compelling a motive as that of obedience to the Commandment of God. We must speak the truth, not merely because to be dishonest will, sooner or later, bring discredit and disaster, but because it is right. We must be truthful and honest in all our dealings, not simply because if we are not we shall give the Church a bad name and scandalize people, but because God wants us to be just and upright. What merit is there in being honest simply

because we know in that so being we shall best prosper in this world? The fear of disgrace is certainly not a supernatural motive for the practice of any virtue. To be truthful because experience proves that liars are always found out eventually may be worldly wisdom, but it will avail us nothing in the eyes of God.

Peroration: St. Paul gives us, in our text, the true motive for truthfulness, when he reminds us that "we are members one of another." It is the eternal law of charity that admonishes us to be honest lest we inflict an injury upon others. Someone always has to suffer for every lie that is told, and it is not a fact that usually it is someone else than the liar himself? Lying is the refuge of cowards, and it usually puts blame on another. Or it the expression of pride and vanity, which seeks to exalt self above others, generally to their hurt. Either way, the law of charity is broken by a lie, whether it be the love that binds us to God who commands us to speak the truth, or that fraternal charity which forbids us to bear false witness against our neighbor. Lying is always the devil's work, for he is a liar and the father of lies. (St. John 8:44). Of the glory of Heaven it is said in Holy Scripture that "there shall not enter into it any ... that maketh a lie" (Apocalypse 21:27). And among the evil crew that inhabit hell is numbered "every one that loveth and maketh a lie" (Apocalypse 22:15). With these terrible warnings in our ears, shall we not seek our part with those who love and serve God "in deed and in truth" (1 St. John 3:18).

Twentieth Sunday After Pentecost

(Ephesians 5:15 and 16) See how you walk circumspectly, not as unwise, but as wise; redeeming the time, because the days are evil.

Nothing is more foolish than sin; nothing a greater waste of time, of energy, of money; nothing more clearly shows a man to be lacking in the elements of common sense and prudence than to engage in a career of sin. Look at the matter calmly, as you would look at any affair of human business. Is it the part of wisdom to let transitory pleasures interfere with your business? Yet sin interferes seriously with the most important business of all, the great work of saving your soul. We do not need an Apostle to tell us that the days are evil, that temptations abound on every hand, that it is easier, on account of our fallen nature, to fall into sin than to stand upright in virtue. We shall be wise, we shall be advised, if we take a little time to consider this matter carefully.

(1) What does sin cost you? For sin, of any kind, is an expensive luxury. We do not always have to pay in money for sin, though often times it makes a big hole in our pocket books. For example: how much does it cost to commit the sin of gluttony? Or to make arrangements for the unlawful satisfaction of any bodily lust? Pride, and its weak sister, vanity, lure many dollars out of our purses. Sin costs money, but even those sins that do not have to be paid for in coin take their toll of our resources of brain and body. Sin is always excess, and for excess the sinner must always pay in loss of strength, impaired alertness, the lessening esteem of his fellows, perhaps the withdrawal of their confidence and altogether, the consequent

loss of opportunities. Worst of all sin, persisted in and repented, costs you the loss of God and of Heaven. Is sin worth the price you pay for it?

(2) What does sin get you? Some of the results of it we have considered already. But they are not the results that we think of when we are tempted. Then we can only see what seems to be the advantage of sin: the pleasure it will bring, the titillation of our senses, the gratification of our pride, the social prestige, the business gain, the place and prominence and power that we think will be ours if we yield to the voice of the deceiver. But experience should have shown us long ago that the devil deserves his title of father of lies, for when has sin actually brought us all that temptation promised? Have the pleasures of sin ever been as keen as anticipation painted them, the advantages of dishonesty, or pride, or violence ever measured up to what we expected of them beforehand? We can be certain of one thing when we sin and that is—disappointment. Once again the devil has made fools of us! We have nothing but that to show for the price we have paid for our sin. But, unless we repent and forsake our sin, we shall have something more to show for it. "The wages of sin is death" (Romans 6:23). In the end that is all that sin gets us.

(3) What folly, then to spend time, energy, money for sin! No man in his better moments but will admit that no sin is worth the price he has to pay for it, either in this world or the next. It is, then, a plain matter of prudent common sense to avoid sin, nothing more than the part of wisdom to live a good and virtuous life. All this is very easy to see, very easy to say, but very hard to do. But common sense will also show us ways of doing it. One of them is indicated in our text. It is to keep busy with good deeds and so crowd out the evil which presses upon us. Most sins are begotten of idleness, which is itself a sin. Not always physical idleness, though this is a most prolific breeding-ground for those temptations which pertain especially to

the flesh; but mental and spiritual idleness which fosters the growth of sins of thought and the graver sins of pride, avarice and envy. The wise man, who wishes above everything else to save his soul active, lest he succumb to the evil which on every side seeks to lure him from the path of virtue. He will look about him and see what sin has brought to others. He will recollect himself and see what his own experience of sin should teach him. And then, he will get busy!

Peroration: Just as a man must be prudent, alert, watchful, if he wishes to make a success of the worldly business which brings him his livelihood; as he will be diligent, self-denying, enthusiastic in carrying out his projects; so in the business of saving his soul he will bring forth the same qualities, make the same or even greater efforts, display the same zeal. Only it will all be from a supernatural motive and directed towards a supernatural end. And in this spiritual business he will have helps that he will not have in his worldly efforts. In them he must rely largely on his native cleverness, his skill in his trade, his keenness of vision, his calm business judgment. But in this supernatural competition with the enemies of his soul, he would certainly find himself unable to cope successfully with the odds against him were it not for the aid of divine grace. But the bestowal of that grace will depend largely on his own effo ts, for it is very true that God helps those who help themselves, and the basis of most supernatural gifts is nature. The e is no question but that this work will be successful if he uses the combination of his own will, plus the grace of God. The e is no question but that he will fail if he trusts solely to himself. Failures in business cost us money, so we learn by our mistakes. Shall we be less wise in our spiritual affairs?

Twenty-First Sunday After Pentecost

(Ephesians 6:11) Put you on the armor of God, that you may be able to stand against the deceits of the devil.

St. Paul enumerates the various parts of this spiritual armor:—the girdle of truth about the loins, the breastplate of justice, the footgear of the gospel of peace, the helmet of salvation, the sword of the spirit, and, above all, the shield of Faith. The imagery is that of the fully armed legionary in heavy marching order and ready at the call of the trumpet to go into battle and win the fight. That this is no mere poetical figure of speech, but intensely practical advice for us in our every-day battle against temptation, which should appear at once if we give the matter the study it deserves. For the Apostle is writing of that spiritual combat in which every one of us is forced to engage if we have any interest at all in the salvation of our souls. There are only two classes of people who have no fight with evil: Those who are so indifferent that they do not care whether they save their souls or not (and, terrible to think, there are such); and those who have so far surrendered to the enemy of souls that they no longer struggle. God grant none of us belong to either class, but that we are all of those good soldiers of Christ, who in Confirmation have enrolled themselves to fight the good fight till death.

(1) What, then, is the spiritual equipment for this life-long battle against sin? It is not a natural panoply, for our battle is against supernatural forces, yes against the devil himself, and against those inclinations of our nature which would betray us

into his hands. Important as the other articles of our spiritual armor may be, St. Paul gives first place to Faith. Not any sort of Faith, certainly not mere credulity, but the faith. For our holy Religion not only teaches us what we must believe in order to save our souls, but what we must do, and not do, in order to practice our Faith. The devil is a doubter, and he tries to make us doubt in order that he may deprive us of our surest defense against the temptations he hurls against us. Uncertainty with regard to religious truth is his most potent weapon, for it disarms us and leaves us defenceless against his assaults. You can easily see how this is so. The widespread immorality of our day is attributable to nothing so much as to the vague and uncertain attitude of the modern mind regarding Religion. If a man does not believe in a future life of rewards and punishments, or if his ideas on these truths are not reasoned out and guided by revelation, he very soon comes to the point where he is ready to say "What's the use? The future life is very problematical. I may as well get all I can out of this one."

(2) To have a definite and certain Faith is the surest way to live a good life. For Faith does govern conduct, and the cry, "It does not matter what a man believes so long as he does what is right," is a bit of sophistry which any thinking man should see through in an instant. How can I do what is right, when I do not know what right is? How can I do what is right, when my belief leads me to accept as right what is really wrong? I may be (for example) a Socialist, and honestly believe that there should be no such thing as private property. I have a right to my opinion. But if I act on it, I shall land in jail! I may believe that if it is a good thing to have one wife, it is much better to have two or three. But if I carry my belief into practice, I shall not be living a good life, and even the law of this world will condemn me.

Then, too, experience should teach us to distrust our own judgment where it has to do with our own case. Inclination is not a proper guide to conduct, and society would soon be disrupted if every man did as he thought best for himself. There must be a common standard of right and wrong, equally binding upon all, and that can only come from a definite, revealed and true Faith.

(3) But the Faith is something more than a guide to right living, something more than a plan of campaign against evil. If it were only a matter of knowing what is right, the problem would indeed be easy. But it is more than an intellectual affair, it is a practical business, and it is a fight which, experience shows us again and again, we simply cannot win in our own strength. But our Faith, our holy Religion, brings to us the supernatural assistance which alone can assure the victory. If the fight were simply against natural odds, we might have some hope that enlightened intelligence, strength of character in the natural virtues, the example of great and good men, the rewards of this world would bring us safely through. But supernatural dangers, supernatural assaults, a supernatural enemy, must be met by supernatural means, hence the Sacraments.

Peroration: The other parts of the Christian armor are only less important than the shield of Faith. Only lack of time prevents us from considering them in detail. Truth, justice, peace, are only possible in conjunction with Faith, as salvation and the life of the spirit are dependent upon it. Together they are (we say it with all reverence) an unbeatable combination, an impregnable armor. And they are ours! Did we but make full use of them, we should never fall into sin. Did we but fight with them we should never be overcome.

Twenty-Second Sunday After Pentecost

(Philippians 1:6) Brethren, we are confident in the Lord Jesus, that he who hath begun a good work in you will perfect it unto the day of the Lord Jesus.

Perseverance! What a world of meaning is in that word! In no sense is it more important than its religious and spiritual connotation, for it is upon our final perseverance that our eternal salvation depends. We cannot merit a good death; we can only, by the grace of God, live the kind of life which God will reward by the gift of final perseverance. The e is nothing God wishes more than that we should be saved; there is nothing we should wish and pray for more fervently, work for with more zeal, and, if we do our part, expect more confidentl . Because there can be no possible doubt that God will do His part in the great and lifelong work of saving our souls.

(1) At the font of Baptism, God begins the good work of grace, by raising our souls to the supernatural order, bestowing upon them the priceless heritage of sanctifying grace, infusing into them the theological virtues of Faith, Hope, and Charity. All this is done without any desert of ours, indeed we deserve nothing from God, for we enter the world with the taint of original sin upon us, and can claim, as our right, no slightest gift or consideration from God. But His love and His mercy, at the very outset, change all this in a wonderful way, transform us from mere creatures, already in debt to our Creator, to the status of sons, sons of God and heirs of His Kingdom, as we are taught in Holy Scripture. In most cases this miracle of grace is wrought in our souls without any coöperation on our part, for we receive Baptism in earliest

infancy, and it is only later on that we are called upon to make use of the grace bestowed upon us, to correspond with it, to treasure and preserve it by every effort of which we are capable.

(2) But God is not content with simply beginning the good work of grace in our souls: He continues, all through our life, to shower us with blessings and favors. Even when, by sin, we forfeit the grace already given, He stands ready to restore to us the heritage we have willfully lost, though in order that we might have such superabundant benefits it was necessary for our Blessed Lord to die upon the Cross. The Sacraments of Holy Church are always open to us, and when we most need the help of God, we find it in them. Confirmation to strengthen us as childhood gives way to the increasing temptations of youth. The Blessed Sacrament, ever and always, whatever the exigency or the need, to flood our souls with grace sufficien to bring us in triumph through any and all temptations, to soothe all sorrows, to make endurable any circumstances. Confession, again and again, to bring back to us God's friendship, and to help us against relapse. Special Sacramental helps for special states of life. Matrimony when that important step is to be taken; Holy Orders for those whom God calls to be the spiritual leaders of His people. Unction when the spark of life is flicke - ing low and we dare not face the darkness and dread of death without God's grace. So He, who began the good work in our souls at the font, continues it to the very edge of the grave.

(3) Besides Sacramental grace, there are the innumerable graces, blessings and favors which God showers upon us every day of our life, if we are in the condition of friendship with Him. Yes, and even when we become His enemies by sin, even then, though we have flouted, insulted, denied Him, He gives us, if we will but avail ourselves of it, the actual grace to repent and come back to Him. Does a sudden crisis arise (not neces-

sarily one in which sin is involved) He offers us the graces we need to meet it. Are we sore beset by temptation; His grace will make issue, a way of escape that we may be enabled to turn it into victory. Most of these graces are literally "ours for asking," for God bestows them in answer to prayer. The protection of Divine Providence; the averting of dangers that threaten us; the lights and guiding of the Holy Spirit; the ordering of circumstances to our souls' good; these, and many other favors, are the way of Grace in us, will perfect it unto the end if we do our part.

Peroration: For as it is true that without God we can do nothing, so it is true that without our coöperation God will do little or nothing for us. His gifts are conditioned. Even the grace of the Sacraments, which works of its own power, will turn against us to our loss unless we receive it worthily and make use of it. So perseverance is, to a very large degree, our task, our responsibility. We cannot doubt but that God will help us to the last, yet neither can we believe that without our acceptance and use of His graces they will avail us anything. Our effo t is essential to final perseverance, our faithfulness in the reception and appropriation of grace, both Sacramental and actual, is a sine qua non in the great work of saving our souls, which we are admonished by St. Paul to prosecute in fear and trembling. We must never forget that it is possible that we may be lost. But we must never forget, either, that if we do our part, as good, practical, fervent Catholics, making regular and frequent use of the Sacraments and prayer, fighting with all our will against temptation and sin, we may be confident that we shall be saved. This is not the mechanical arrangement that the enemies of the Church would represent it to be. It is merely that certitude of faith without which there can be no spiritual quietude and security.

Twenty-Third Sunday After Pentecost

(Philippians 3:20) But our conversation is in heaven...

Both in the literal and in the modern meaning of the word "conversation" may be found useful lessons. At the time when the Vulgate was translated into English at Douay, "conversation" meant a man's entire manner of life. Since then the word has become limited to matters of speech. So our consideration of the text divides itself, without at all contradicting the essential meaning of the Apostle.

We are reminded, again and again, in the Epistles no less than in the Gospels, that we are citizens of the Kingdom of Heaven; that though we must live in this world, we are not to live as worldlings. The motives which underlie our life and action must be supernatural, and our actions themselves are limited by the laws, not of earth, but of Heaven, for which this life here is but a trial and a preparation. What we may and may not do is clearly marked out for us by our holy Religion, even what we may say and not say, what we may think and not think. Nor is this an intolerable serfdom, which robs us of liberty of thought and action, and enchains both intellect and will. Rather it is the way to true freedom, a beneficent legislation, which protects us on every side, and by directing us to the path of safety, sets our feet on the road which leads to happiness not only hereafter but in this world here and now.

(1) "The world is too much with us," says the poet, and its insistent claims upon our attention and interest are not likely to be forgotten. We have to be reminded frequently that not

only is this world not all, but it is, in comparison with the world to come, only important insofar as it serves to advance our interests in the Kingdom of Heaven. Merely in the matter of time, it is evident that this is true, for while we may spend some three score and ten years here, we are destined to spend an endless eternity in Heaven, or (which may God forbid) in hell. Which it will be, depends upon how we spend the few brief years of trial here in this world, for God has seen fit to decree that upon our life in the flesh shall depend our everlast-ing destiny. We are warned in Holy Scripture that we are but pilgrims and sojourners, transients, visitors, in this world; and we must never forget what is the real business of life, whither we are going, and what the end of it all will be.

(2) Were it not for this knowledge of our eternal destiny, this life would be meaningless, nay more, it would be an intolerable burden. How account for the troubles and sorrows of life, except in the light of eternity, where patient suffering will redound to the merit of our immortal souls? How bear the injustices and inequalities of our miserable human existence, except in view of the everlasting rewards promised to those who endure to the end? Without the promise of Heaven to those who are faithful to God and do right in this life, who would be able to face the temptations and trials which daily beset us? So our life ought to be lived in the constantly recurring thought of Heaven, as the end to which we tend, and in comparison with which everything that happens to us in this life is only import-ant insofar as it helps or hinders our progress to our goal.

(3) The modern meaning of the word "conversation" has also its lesson for us, and a very practical lesson it is. Though we understand the importance of saving our souls, how very seldom we speak of the things that pertain to our spiritual life! It is not always reverence which holds us silent. We naturally speak most of the things which interest us most, which we consider most important. If there is so little religious conversation

in our homes, between friends, or at various crises of our life, it can only be because we fail to realize the religious bearing of these things. If there is a prejudice against what we call "pious talk," it is largely for the reason that we feel, somehow, a certain sense of unreality in such speech, or are afraid that others will set us down as devotees. The result is that we are as reticent about our religion as we are about our bank balance, and though religion is the most important thing in our life, we hardly ever refer to it even in our most intimate conversations with our nearest and dearest. It was not always so among Catholics. Religious references used to be part of the daily life of our ancestors, and no one thought them "pious" in the sense of insincerity.

But, on the other hand, our conversation is full of matters which ought never to be even mentioned by Catholic Christians. The e is plenty of scandal talked over, plenty of vulgar and obscene conversation, plenty of idle and vain boasting, plenty of unjust criticism, and all of these things are positively wrong and wicked. Such conversation is surely not "in Heaven," as the Apostle would say; rather it is, if not of hell itself, at least of the earth earthy. This is not good religion, it is not even good manners, for such things are beneath the dignity of Christian men and women, and should be avoided, not only because they are sinful, but because they are vulgar.

Peroration: If we would but refer every thought, word, and action to the fact that we are seeking first and in everything to save our souls, how much happier we should be, how much better, how much more respected, how much more useful! To have a good and religious motive for everything we do will not make us any the less efficient or successful in the affair of this world. The most practical man is he who conducts his affairs according to the dictates of the moral law, with regard to justice, honesty, and the rights of others. The man or woman whose "conversation" is never offensive, has more friends, real friends, than the person whose speech reeks of the gutter. We need to understand that we can save our souls without foregoing even one of the truly desirable things of this life, indeed that by using this world, as it was meant to be used, enjoying its benefits as they were meant to be used, not abused, we can make of this world a ladder which will bring us to heaven. Only so can we be happy here, only so can we attain happiness hereafter.

Twenty-Fourth and Last Sunday After Pentecost

(Colossians 1:14) In whom we have redemption through His blood, the remission of sins.

We owe the salvation of our immortal souls, even the possibility of salvation, to none other than Jesus Christ. Were it not for Him, His love and His mercy, His life and His death, we would not even have a chance of winning Heaven. For we are human creatures, members of a race which rebelled against God in its very beginning, and has been turning away from Him ever since. We come into this life in the natural order, with no claim whatever upon God for any happiness in this world or the next. And though He raises us, in Baptism, to the supernatural state of sanctifying grace, and gives us actual grace in abundance, we fling this priceless heritage away, and go through life from one sin to another. Heaven! Salvation! What is there in us to merit it? Were it not for Jesus Christ, who could even imagine it possible?

(1) So great was the sin of our First Parents, so innumerable were the actual sins of mankind, so terrible our own disobedience against the known laws of God, that nothing less than the death of Christ, true God and true Man, could purchase for us redemption and salvation. No mere man, however good, could have atoned for one mortal sin, to say nothing of the sins of the whole world. It is dreadful thing to think of what would have become of us, if God had not taken pity, and sent His only Son into the world to live and die for us. Only God could

be so loving, so generous, after the way in which mankind had repaid Him for all His blessings and favors. God had the right to take vengeance on the world for its wickedness; He chose rather to save it. We had no right whatever to expect anything from God; but He gives us everything!

(2) Judge of the malice of mortal sin by the price God had to pay to redeem us from its consequences. We underestimate the wickedness of sin, for we have become used to it; it is so frightfully common in the world, even in our own lives, that we do not regard it with the shrinking horror it deserves. We see the temporal results of sin all around us,—disgrace, sorrow, sickness, death. But even these dreadful things we take as a matter of course, and do not refer them to their real cause. Of the eternal consequences of sin we can have but the vaguest notion, but even from that we turn away, and the word hell, the most dreadful word in all our language, is lightly used, as if it meant nothing at all. From childhood we are so accustomed to sin that we condone it in others and plunge into it ourselves with hardly a thought of what it means to our souls, thinking only of the advantage, or the pleasure, which it deceitfully promises us.

(3) But if we look at Jesus Christ, paying the price for sin upon the Cross, then we may form some slight conception of what it should mean to us, by realizing what it means to God. Look at the Crucifix. See our dear Lord in agony unspeakable; watch Him die alone, forsaken, derided. That is what sin means to God. That is what my sin means to Jesus Christ. For if I alone, of all who have every lived or will live, from the beginning of the world to the end of time, had committed one mortal sin, that would have been necessary to redeem me, and bring to me the remission of my sin! For blood is the price of Heaven, only by the Cross would God take away the blacker stain of sin. Shall I, then, sin carelessly, lightly, wilfully? Shall I dare to sin at all? Am I one of those who regard sin as of no

consequence, a pitiable human weakness, an uncontrollable disease, an irresistible weakness? I am hard enough on others when they go wrong, but oh, so easy on myself when I am the sinner! How I seek to excuse myself, to palliate my guilt, to avoid my responsibility. Worst of all, how I delay my penitence, taking the fearful chance of dying in sin and thus losing my soul forever, when the means of pardon and absolution are so easily available.

Peroration: Daily the good Catholic protests that he loves Jesus Christ above all things. Is this avowal more than mere lip service? Daily we cry to God for mercy and forgiveness of our sins. Are we really sincere in our repentance for past misdeeds? Every time we make an act of contrition we swear to God that we will do everything in our power to amend our lives, avoid the occasions of sin, yes we even promise that we will sin no more. Do we mean what we say? Actions speak louder than words. It is for us to prove to God and to ourselves that we are not speaking words that mean nothing. It is for us to show our gratitude to our Blessed Lord for what He has done for our souls, by setting ourselves, with the help of His grace, to live godly, just, and sober lives. For that Redemption, which was purchased by Him upon the Cross of His bitter pain is not alone the blotting out of what has been; it is the strength in which we may reform our lives; it gives the grace without which we can do nothing. Shall we, then, sin again and lose all this?

–Finis–

www.ingramcontent.com/pod-product-compliance
Lightning Source LLC
Chambersburg PA
CBHW030522080526
44586CB00011B/295